NEEDLEPLAY

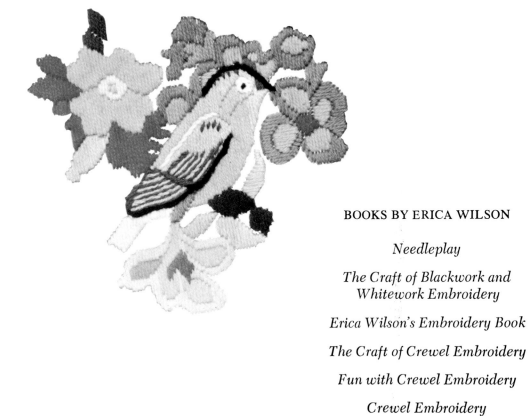

BOOKS BY ERICA WILSON

Needleplay

*The Craft of Blackwork and
Whitework Embroidery*

Erica Wilson's Embroidery Book

The Craft of Crewel Embroidery

Fun with Crewel Embroidery

Crewel Embroidery

NEEDLEPLAY

ERICA WILSON

CHARLES SCRIBNER'S SONS / NEW YORK

This book is dedicated to the great team
at the W. G. B. H. television station in Boston

I would like to express my thanks and gratitude to all my co-workers in Boston, New York and Nantucket who helped to make the book possible: Rick Hauser, Margaret McLeod, James Field, Eleanor Jones, David Atwood, Fran Mahard, Conrad White, Pauline Mercer, Dia Wasley, Alison Lerch, Lindsay Green, Donna Rothchild, Nancy Sussan, and of course my indefatigable editor, Elinor Parker.

All the photographs were taken by Michel Tcherevkoff except those on pages 74, 78, and 88, which were taken by Vladimir Kagan, and on page 42 which was taken for *House and Garden* magazine by Sol Leiter. Cover photograph: Jack Shipley.

Library of Congress Cataloging in Publication Data

Wilson, Erica.
 Needleplay.
 Includes index.
 1. Embroidery. I. Title.
TT770.W57   746.4′4   75-6036
ISBN 0-684-14362-3

Pictures of books by A. A. Milne are reprinted with the permission of E. P. Dutton & Co., Inc. and are from the following titles: THE HOUSE AT POOH CORNER, copyright 1928 by E. P. Dutton & Co., copyright renewed 1956 by A. A. Milne; WHEN WE WERE VERY YOUNG, copyright 1924 by E. P. Dutton & Co., copyright renewed 1952 by A. A. Milne; WINNIE-THE-POOH, copyright 1926 by E. P. Dutton & Co., copyright renewed 1954 by A. A. Milne. Illustrated by Ernest H. Shepard.
The embroideries shown on pages 151, 165, 330 and 331 and color plate 28 are adapted from illustrations by Beatrix Potter in THE TALE OF TWO BAD MICE, APPLEY DAPPLY'S NURSERY RHYMES and THE TALE OF JOHNNY TOWN-MOUSE and are reproduced by kind permission of Frederick Warne and Company Limited.
An illustration by Ernest H. Shepard from THE WIND IN THE WILLOWS by Kenneth Grahame is reprinted with the permission of Charles Scribner's Sons, copyright © 1959 Ernest H. Shepard.

1 3 5 7 9 11 13 15 17 19 MYD/C 20 18 16 14 12 10 8 6 4 2

PRINTED IN THE UNITED STATES OF AMERICA

CONTENTS

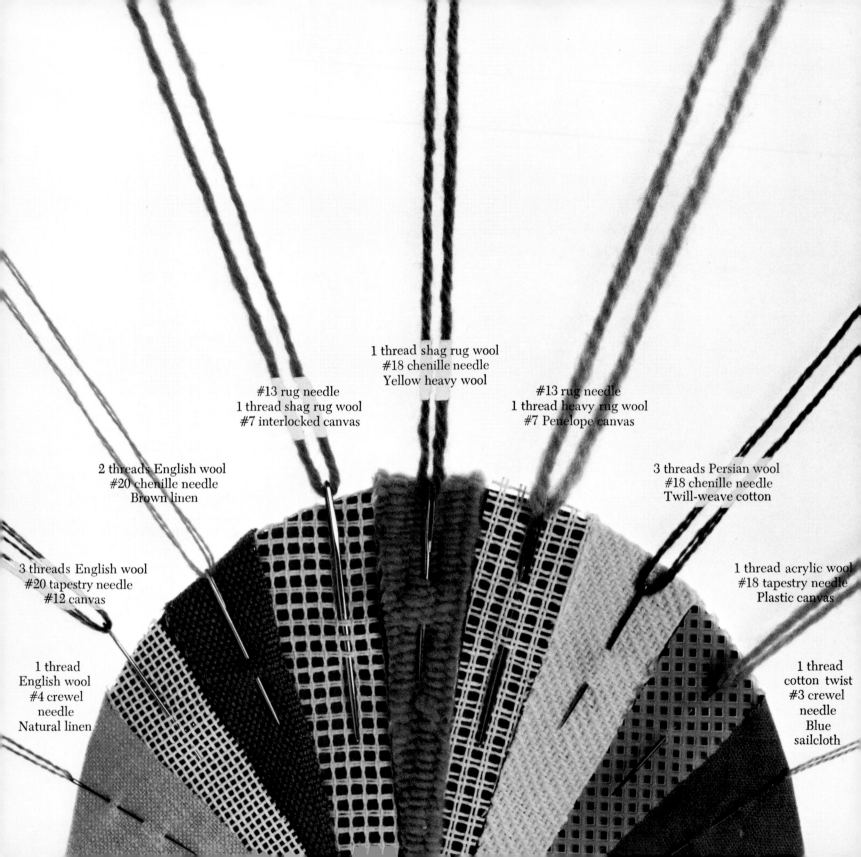

1 thread shag rug wool
#18 chenille needle
Yellow heavy wool

#13 rug needle
1 thread shag rug wool
#7 interlocked canvas

#13 rug needle
1 thread heavy rug wool
#7 Penelope canvas

2 threads English wool
#20 chenille needle
Brown linen

3 threads Persian wool
#18 chenille needle
Twill-weave cotton

3 threads English wool
#20 tapestry needle
#12 canvas

1 thread acrylic wool
#18 tapestry needle
Plastic canvas

1 thread
English wool
#4 crewel
needle
Natural linen

1 thread
cotton twist
#3 crewel
needle
Blue
sailcloth

INTRODUCTION

This book is the outcome of my series of twenty-six programs on Public Television. Each one covered a different subject and each one was designed to show how varied and unlimited ideas for stitchery can be. You can make a friend that perfect gift no one else can give her (or him!), personalize something of your own, make anything from a giant wall tapestry to a miniature pincushion, a place mat, or a pot holder, a bolster or a bedspread. There's nothing that equals the satisfaction of making something all yourself—as any "super-stitcher" will tell you . . . and you'll surely find it more like needleplay than needlework!

The materials you will need are relatively simple. A needle, naturally, some wool, cotton or acrylic threads, the background fabric, a couple of thimbles, scissors, and there you are. The only other thing you will need is some way to stretch the fabric taut, so that your stitching will be smooth and even, and easy to do. The various solutions to that are shown on the next pages.

FRAMES

Most needlework, crewel, needlepoint, and silk embroidery are easier and better worked if the background fabric is stretched taut. Illustrated here are various types of frames with stands and supports that allow you to work with both hands free—one above and one below the frame. In this way you can work smoothly with even rhythm just like the professionals. It is essential to have the fabric stretched really tightly in order to keep the stitches even.

LEFT TO RIGHT:

Standing floor frame with 12″ hoop

36″ oval rug frame

Stretcher strip frame
  (available in ½″ modules)

Lap or "fanny" frame with 10″ hoop

(Hoops and bases of the "fanny" and
  floor frames are interchangeable.)

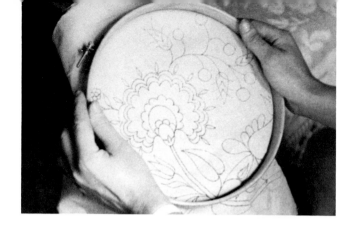

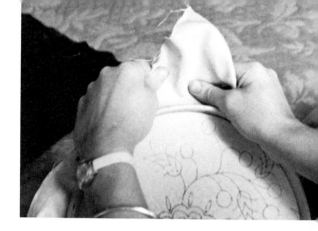

MOUNTING THE MATERIAL
INTO A RING FRAME

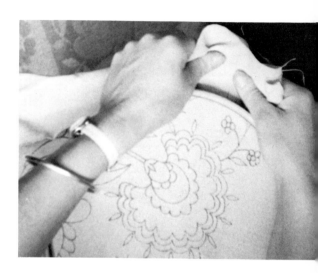

First remove the outer hoop of the frame. Lay the material over the inner ring with that part of the design that is to be worked exposed in the center. Tighten the screw of the outer hoop (*before* placing it in position), adjusting it so that it fits down over both the inner ring and the material very snugly. Do not press the hoop all the way down—just push it on so that it fits firmly all around (as shown in the first photo).

The next step is to pull the fabric taut while simultaneously pressing down on the rim of the frame with your palms (as shown in the next two photos). Work right round the perimeter in this way until the material is stretched like a drum. Finally, press down the outer hoop. It need not be absolutely flat as long as the material is taut.

The last photo shows the right hand underneath the frame passing the needle through to the left hand on top. *Always* keep the same hand underneath the frame and pass the needle vertically through the fabric to the other hand on top. Continue, passing it back and forth vertically in this way, never changing the position of your hands.

To remove the hoop, simply press down on the embroidery with your thumbs, simultaneously lifting off the hoop with your fingers. Do not attempt to alter the screw adjustment before removing it.

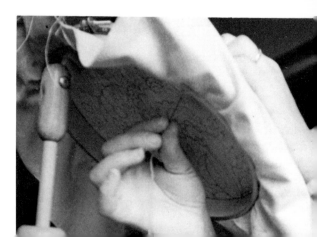

THREADING THE NEEDLE

Here is the easiest way to thread soft wool into a long-eyed needle.

1. Wrap thread round the needle as shown.

2. Hold thread tightly, close around needle, grasping the thread between the fleshy part of finger and thumb, not near the nail. Pull needle away.

3. Squeeze thread *tightly* between finger and thumb, so that thread is almost buried. Press the eye of the needle flat on to the thread, rather than attempting to push the thread through the needle. Pull through when the amount of thread shown in the photo has appeared (Figure 3).

4. Success! If at first you don't succeed, practice with a huge rug needle and strands of crewel wool . . . and don't forget to squeeze the thread as tightly as if it were a flea about to jump!

YOUR LIBRARY OF CREWEL STITCHES

On the following pages you will find your library of crewel stitches. They are called "crewel" because most of the basic ones were traditionally used in wool embroidery. This is not to say that you can't use them with all sorts of threads, from rug wool to finest silks or cotton. If you have not tried them out before, it is quite a difficult undertaking to hunt through your "library" for the perfect stitch to use in a certain design. That's why it is best to make a sampler (like the mirror frame or boxes on pages 126 and 127), or become familiar with the stitches by working them in any of the crewel designs in this book. It's just like learning a language; once you have a vocabulary of stitches at hand, you can apply them imaginatively to any design of your own in all sorts of different ways. In crewel and crewel point, the fun of it all is choosing different stitches; the variety of textures and effects you can get is almost unlimited.

BEGINNING AND ENDING

When working in a frame, it is easier to keep everything on the surface, so beginning and ending off are best done by taking the little back stitches on the right side of your work, as shown here. If you place them on one of the design outlines they will easily be covered later as you continue to work. Turning to the back of your frame to end off by running your thread into the previous stitches is not done unless *absolutely* necessary—*most* unprofessional because it's a waste of time!

Put a knot in the thread and start on the wrong side of the material. As crewel work should always be backed, the wrong side is not of such tremendous importance, though care should be taken to keep the stitches flat, and not to jump too far from place to place without taking a small stitch in between.

End off with 2 small back stitches on an outline or inside the shape of a design which will later be covered. (The stitches in the diagram are enlarged to show clearly . . . . they should be very small.) Come up at A and pull through at B, then bring thread to front of work near by and cut off.

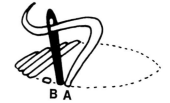

B A

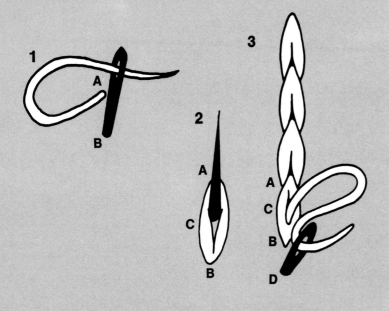

SPLIT STITCH

Like Stem and Chain Stitch, Split Stitch may be worked in close lines all in one direction. It is especially effective worked in one color when the only interest lies in the direction of line. It may be used as an outline stitch but it is more useful as an underlying padding on an edge which will later be covered with other stitching.

1. Needle comes up at A, goes down at B.

2. Needle comes up at C piercing through center of stitch from below, splitting it exactly in the middle.

3. Needle goes down at D, a little ahead of B (the distance from C to D is the same as the length of the first stitch; from A to B). Repeat in this way, forming a smooth line of stitching slightly shortening the stitches when going around curves.

BACKSTITCH

Come up at A, go down at B, then up ahead at C. Repeat, going back into same hole as the previous stitch. Keep all stitches the same size.

THREADED BACKSTITCH

Work a line of Back Stitch, and using a blunt needle and contrasting color, thread it through as shown. The needle passes under the first Back Stitch from right to left (not into the material), through the second Back Stitch from left to right, and so on. Do not draw the interlacing thread too tightly or the effect will be lost.

STEM STITCH

1. Needle comes up at A, goes in at B, and up again at C, exactly half way between A and B. Draw through, holding the thread to the left of the needle.

2. Needle goes in at D, up again at B (in the same hole made by the thread going in previously at B). Draw through, still holding thread to left of needle.

3. Continue by repeating #2. The thread may be held either to the right or the left of the needle, but should remain on the same side once the work is started.

RAISED STEM STITCH

Though it is shown here as a banding stitch, Raised Stem may be used to fill whole areas. In this case the long basic stitches should be tacked down invisibly here and there, afterwards. The stitch may be shaded, working in vertical bands, or stripes of contrasting colors. When used to fill an uneven area it usually needs an outline of Stem Stitch.

1. First work a series of parallel stitches (just under ¼″ apart, as shown in diagram). *To work a wider area than the one shown, lay these lines across the whole width of the shape.*

2. Using a blunt (tapestry) needle, come up at A, and holding thread to left of needle slide under first thread from B to C. Do not go through material.

3. Repeat #2, sliding needle under thread from D to E, and work up to top of thread in this way.

4. Work several lines close side by side always beginning again at the bottom, working upwards until base threads are entirely covered. Do not pack too many rows in, however, or the effect will be lost.

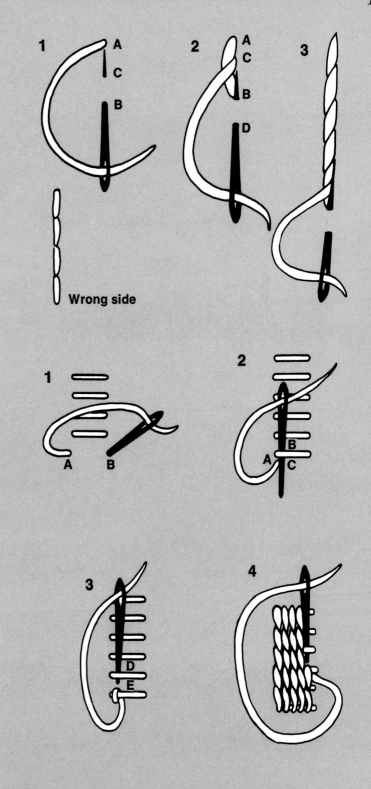

Wrong side

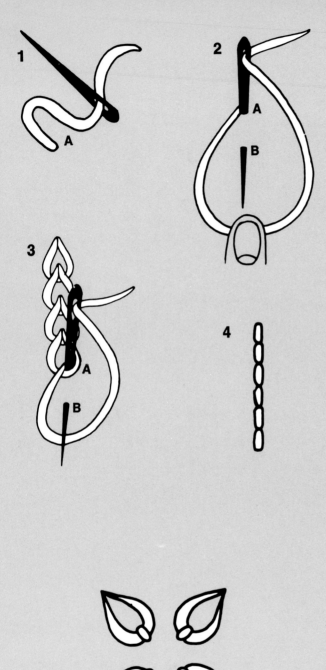

CHAIN STITCH

Chain Stitch may be used as a solid filling, working row upon row closely side by side. Do not pack the stitches *too* closely, however, or the effect will be lost. The filling is equally effective if the lines are shaded, or worked all in one color with contrasting outline. (The stitches should all begin at the same end and run in the same direction to make a smooth effect.) When extra lines have to be added to broaden the shape in one place, add them on the inside, allowing a continuous line to run along the edges. In this way the joining lines will not be obvious, especially if the first stitch of the joining line is tucked *underneath* the longer line.

Chain Stitch may also be used as an outline where a fairly broad dominant edge is needed.

1. Bring needle up at A.

2. Form a loop, and put the needle in at A again, holding loop down with finger. Then come up at B, directly below A. Draw gently through, forming the first chain stitch.

3. Repeat #2, always inserting needle exactly where the thread came out, *inside* the last loop—come up directly below, and draw through so chain stitches lie flat on material. When filling a shape by working rows of Chain Stitch, always work in same direction, beginning each new row at top and working down.

4. Wrong side.

DETACHED CHAIN STITCH

Make a single Chain Stitch and anchor it down with a small stitch (as at the end of a row of Chain Stitch). This stitch may be used as a filling, combined with cross bars, or scattered over the ground as a "powdering" like seeding.

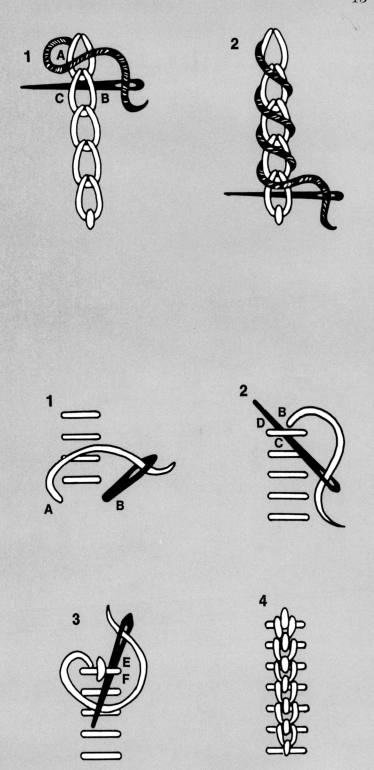

WHIPPED CHAIN STITCH

1. First work a row of chain stitch. Then change to a blunt tapestry needle, come up at A, and slide needle through from B to C. Pick up the chain stitches only, do not go through the material.

2. Continue, sliding the needle lightly under each chain, without pulling the thread too tightly. The finished effect should be like a raised cord.

RAISED CHAIN STITCH

1. First work a series of parallel stitches (just under ¼″ apart) as shown in diagram. (As for Raised Stem Stitch.)

2. Then bring thread up at B and slide under thread from C to D (do not go through material). This stitch is best worked with a blunt needle. Draw through and hold thread upwards keeping it rather taut.

3. Next slide needle downwards under same thread, but to the right of first stitch, from E to F, draw through, holding thread under needle; do not pull too tightly so the appearance of the stitch is as in #4.

4. Continue stitch by repeating #2 and #3. Several rows may be worked side by side to fill a space (as in Raised Stem Stitch) instead of single row shown. In this case end off row at base and start again at the top, ready to work downwards.

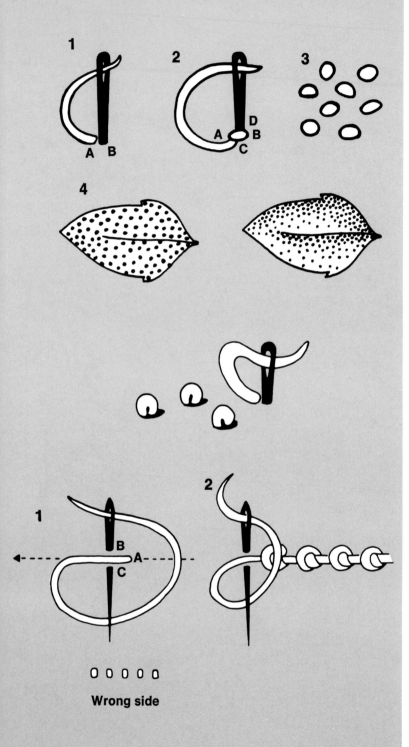

Wrong side

SEEDING

1. Come up at A, and go down at B a small distance away. Pull through, lightly.

2. Come up at C and go down at D, across the first stitch, diagonally. Pull through, so that the stitch forms a firm, round, slightly raised "bump" on the fabric.

3. The finished effect appears as one raised stitch instead of two. When worked with thread which matches the background fabric in color seeding gives an attractive texture effect.

4. Stitches scattered evenly, each slanting in a different direction.

5. Stitches massed closely to form a shaded effect.

RAISED SEEDING

Work seeding but leave each stitch loose to form a raised "bump" on the fabric. As in looped stem the thickness of the thread will hold the seed stitch in place.

CORAL STITCH

The knots may be spaced closely or far apart, but should always be at right angles to the line. When several rows are worked close together the stitches should be fitted into the spaces between the knots on the previous lines. The effect of the stitching when it is solid is almost like rows of fat French Knots. To make it effective it is best to use double thread.

1. Bring needle up at A, lay thread flat in direction of working (indicated by dotted line). Needle then goes in at B, and up at C at right angles to the thread. Holding the thread under needle (as in diagram), draw through and pull gently up to form a knot. The space between B and C determines the size of the knot.

2. Next stitch repeats #1 a little distance away. (The stitch is more effective if the knots are fairly close together.)

BUTTONHOLE STITCH

This is one of the most versatile of stitches. It may be worked in solid rows, or radiating from one central point to form a circle, in scallops, or with the spokes outwards as an outline around a shape.

1. Needle comes up at A, goes in at B, and up at C directly below B, and level with A. Thread is held under needle as in diagram. Draw through downwards.

2. Next stitch repeats #1 at an even distance apart. Stitching may be spaced as shown, or worked closely as in #3.

BULLION KNOTS

Double thread is usually best for this stitch. The knots may be used individually, or worked side by side. They should not be too long, or they will curl instead of lying flat on the material.

1. Bring needle up at A, go down at B, but do not pull thread through.

2. Stab needle up at A again but bring it only *halfway* through material.

3. Holding needle from below, twist thread round needle at A, until number of twists equals the distance between A and B.

4. Holding top of needle and threads firmly with finger and thumb of left hand, draw needle through with right hand, loosening coil of threads with left hand as you do so, to allow needle to pass through freely.

5. Then place needle against end of twist, at the same time pulling on the thread, as shown, until the knot lies flat on the material. If any "bumps" appear in the knot, flatten these by stroking the underneath of twist with the needle, at the same time pulling on the thread.

6. Put needle in close, at the end of the twist, and pull through firmly.

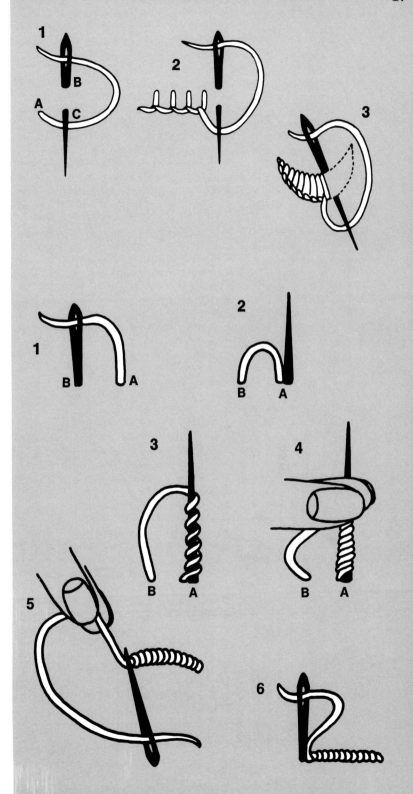

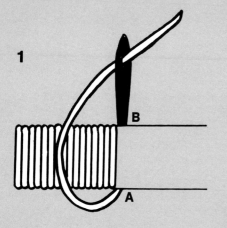

1

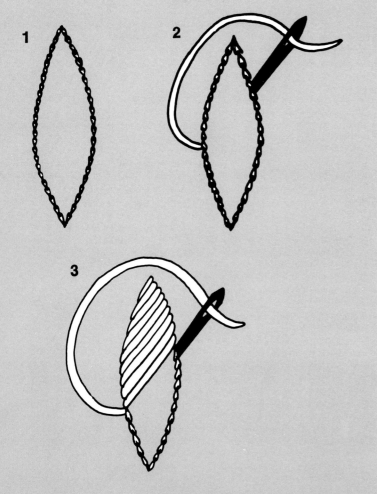

1

2

3

SATIN STITCH

Come up at A and go down at B. Then come up again right next to A, and go down again next to B. Continue, coming up on one side and down on the other to form a smooth band of stitching. The stitches may be straight or slanting but they should always lie evenly side by side.

SLANTING SATIN STITCH

Satin stitch needs practice in order to make it neat and even. A slant helps to make it smoother, and a Split Stitch padding makes it easier to keep the edge clean; both essential to the effect. It should never be used for large areas, because the threads could easily be pulled and disarranged when the embroidery is in use. On very small leaves it is easier to start at the tip and work downwards. To maintain the slant, come up close at the upper edge and go down with a slight space between the stitches on the lower edge. This tends to exaggerate the slant of each stitch but prevents them from flattening out.

1. First outline shape with Split Stitch. (See page 12.)

2. Starting in the center (to be certain of the exact angle), work slanting stitches close together across the shape, coming up and going down *outside* the Split Stitch. (Split Stitch forms a padding on the outline, giving a firm edge.)

3. Work up to tip, then start at center again and finish working shape to the bottom. Stitches should lie evenly side by side, not crowded, but with no material showing between. Do not pull too tightly.

SATIN STITCH/Tied With Back Stitch

This stitch may be used to fill a wider area, for unlike Slanting Satin Stitch, it has a row of stitching to hold it in the center. More than one row of Back Stitch may be worked if the area needs it. Do not pull the Back Stitch too tight for it will spoil the evenness of the Satin Stitch underneath it.

1. Having outlined shape with Split Stitch, Satin Stitch over it, starting in center to guide stitches at the correct angle. Keep stitches fairly upright at outside points (as shown). It is easier to work longer stitches instead of very short ones.

2. As stitches would be too long to leave untied, work a row of Back Stitch through the center of the shape, using the upper edge as a guide line. Needle comes up at A, and down at B, right into the hole made by the last stitch.

PADDED SATIN STITCH

The top row of Padded Satin Stitch may be worked straight instead of slanting, but this is much harder to make even, especially when the stitches are small at the point of a leaf. It is therefore best to practice it on a slant first.

1. Starting in the center of the shape, come up at A, down at B.

2. Fill shape with stitches just side by side.

3. Go across with a few stitches to hold the long ones flat.

4. For the second padding, go up and down vertically again as in #2.

5. Come up at A, down at B, and cover the whole shape with slanting stitches as shown. To maintain the slant, A should always be a fraction ahead of the last stitch, and B should be pushed up very close to the previous stitches. (Otherwise the slant becomes flatter and flatter until it is almost straight.)

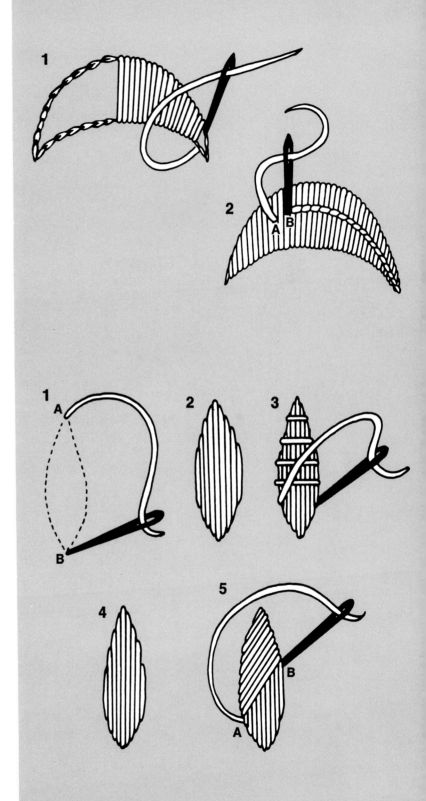

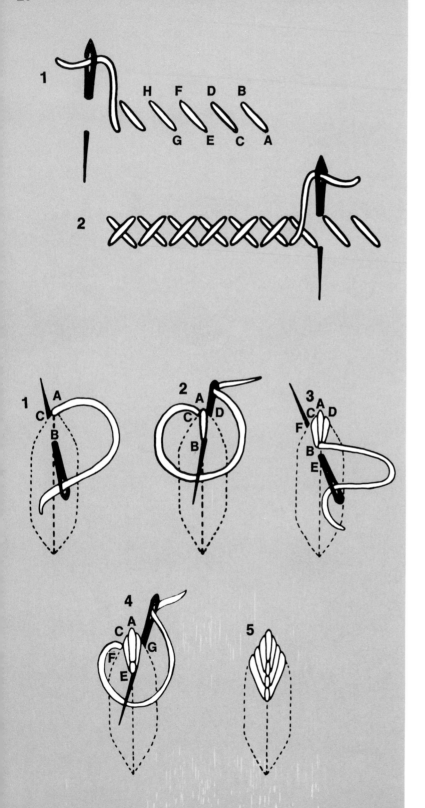

CROSS STITCH

1. Working from right to left, come up at A, go down at B, up at C, and down at D, making a row of slanting stitches. If the needle is always kept vertical and the stitches are spaced evenly apart, the slant of each stitch will always remain the same.

2. Working from left to right, return along the line, again keeping the needle vertical, and going into the exact holes of the first row of slanting stitches. This forms a continuous line of cross stitches as in the diagram. It is important to always keep the final stitch of the cross slanting in the same direction. When blocks of stitches are worked this has a much tidier effect than if some stitches slant from right to left, others from left to right.

FISHBONE STITCH

The first stitch (A to B) should be at least ¼″ long to start the stitch off on a good slant. To maintain this slant, bring the needle up and go down on the edge, almost in the same holes as the previous stitches, and keep the center stitch (B to E) a good length. The stitch looks best if a smooth edge is made which does not need outlining afterwards. Like Cretan, Fishbone may also be worked with spaces between the stitches for an open effect.

1. Come up at A in the center of point. Go down at B directly below it (draw line down center as guide line). Come up at C to left and slightly below A, but touching it, on outline of shape.

2. Go in at D to right and slightly below A, but touching it. Come up at B, and form a loop by holding thread under needle.

3. Draw through and insert needle at E a short space directly below B, come up at F—again to the left and slightly below C, but touching it.

4. Now repeat #2 again; come up at F, go in at G (touching previous threads). Come up at E with thread under the needle. Anchor it down as in #3, and continue in this way.

5. Finished effect.

FRENCH KNOTS

French Knots may be scattered like seeding, to fill an area lightly, or they may be arranged in rows to fill a space solidly. The latter is most effective if each row is clearly defined and the knots lie evenly side by side. Alternatively they may be sprinkled closely but unevenly to produce an intentionally rough surface.

1. Bring needle up at A, twist thread once round needle as shown.

2. Put needle in at A, or just beside it, pull the thread until it fits *closely* round the needle (not too tightly). Pull needle through.

3. The finished knot. The thread should only be twisted once round the needle, as this makes a neat knot; *never* two or three times. The size of the knot is determined by the number of threads and size of the needle used.

FRENCH KNOTS ON STALKS

1. Come up at A, and twist the thread once around the needle as in the diagram. Pull gently, so that the thread fits round the needle, and still holding the thread so it does not loosen, go down at B, about ¼″ away from A.

2. Pull gently through, to form the effect shown.

3. The knots may be used singly, or may be worked to overlap each other. They can be very effective radiating from the center of a circle, as shown here.

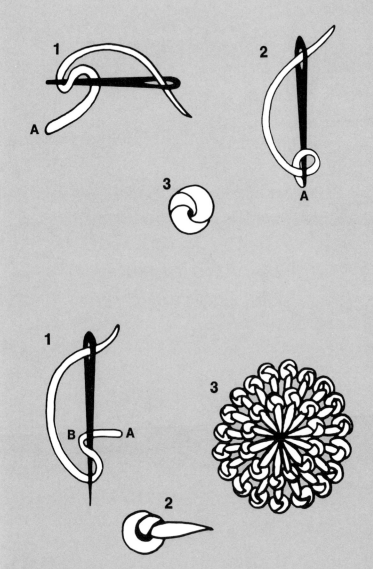

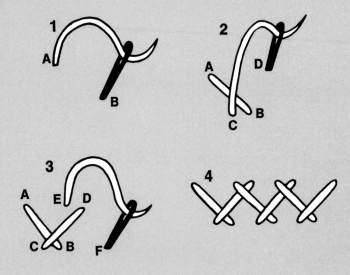

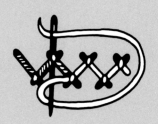

HERRINGBONE STITCH

This stitch is the simple foundation for many variations.

1. Come up at A, go down at B, diagonally below A.

2. Come up at C, little to the left, and level with B, and go down at D, level with A, making a diagonal stitch in the other direction.

3. Come up at E, a little to the left and level with D, go down at F. E to F is another diagonal stitch parallel with A-B. Repeat from #2 again.

4. Continue repeating #2 and #3, spacing the stitches evenly so that the diagonals are parallel.

THREADED HERRINGBONE STITCH

First work a row of Herringbone. With a blunt needle and contrasting color, pick up the under thread of the Herringbone cross, and weave along first the upper, then the lower edge in this way, as shown.

TIED HERRINGBONE STITCH

First work a line of plain Herringbone. With a blunt needle and contrasting thread, slide the needle under the Herringbone cross, pointing the needle towards the center of the line. While needle is held in position, twist thread over and under the needle, as shown. Draw tight to knot it. Work this Coral Knot on each cross along the line, always pointing the needle toward the center of the Herringbone band.

INTERLACED HERRINGBONE STITCH

First work a row of Herringbone. Beginning on the right, with a blunt needle and contrasting thread pick up the first bar of the Herringbone, slanting the needle downwards. Pick up the next bar slanting the needle upwards (direction of needle is indicated by arrows). Continue to the end of the line.

CLOSE HERRINGBONE STITCH

This stitch is smoothest if kept slanting. Space the stitches a little apart when the needle goes down, and keep them close together (almost touching) when the needle comes up on the edge. This will help maintain the slant, and make a sharp V in the center. It is attractive when used on small leaves.

1. Come up at A, go down at B, diagonally below A.

2. Come up at C, go down at D (C is directly below A; D is directly above B).

3. Come up at E, close to A, go down at F, close to B.

4. Come up at G, close to C, go down at H close to D.

5. Continue in this way along the line, forming a solid band of stitching.

CLOSE HERRINGBONE STITCH/Leaf shape

1. Come up at A, about ¼" away from the point of the leaf. Go down at point B. Repeat on opposite side (C to D) making 2 closely crossed stitches.

2. Continue working first one side then the other. Maintain a steep slant by leaving a space each time you come up (between E and A) and go in close at B.

3. Shows finished effect.

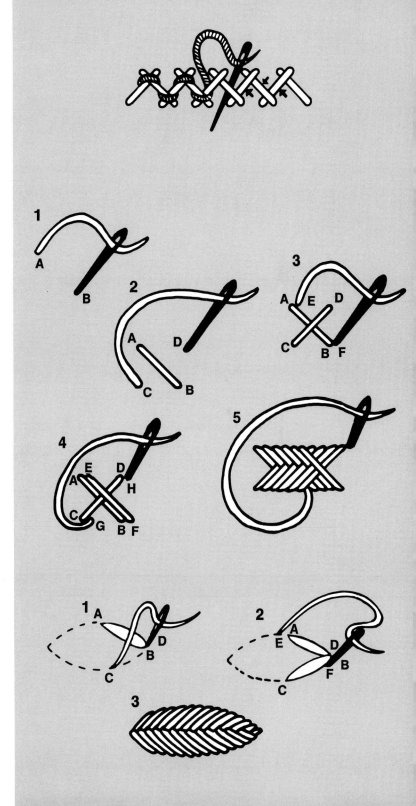

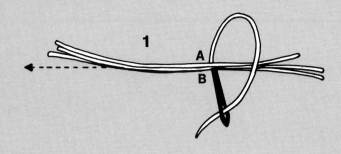

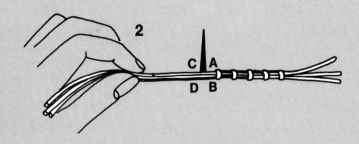

COUCHING

Couching may be worked as a plain outline, having the couching threads the same color as those underneath. Either one or two threads may be used in the needle and any number of threads may be couched down. Or two contrasting colors may be used, and the top stitches worked to form patterns. Couching may be used as a solid filling, working the threads back and forth or round in circles, or following the shape of the motif being filled. It may also be used as an open filling, called Random Couching, and is worked in any direction until the ground is evenly but lightly filled.

1. Lay a bundle of threads (in this case 3) along the line, and with one thread in the needle come up at A, in at B. (B is almost in the same hole as A.)

2. Come up at C, about ¼″ from A-B, down again at D, and continue in this way holding the bundle of threads taut with your left hand as you sew.

3. When the line is completed, thread the 3 threads into a large-eyed needle, plunge them through the material exactly in the hole made by the last couching stitch and cut them off short (about ¼″) on reverse side.

4. Patterns may be made with the couching stitches (brick stitch shown). Always bring needle up on the outside, and go down close to the line already worked, so that no material shows between lines of couching. At the corners work couching stitch at the angle shown to make a sharp corner without having to plunge threads at the end of each line.

Couching in a Circle

Then try couching to fill a circle. With a pencil, lightly draw regularly spaced lines radiating out from the center of the circle, and use these as a guide for your couching stitches. Fold in half one length of gold thread to be used for the couching and start by sewing down the loop end of this doubled thread in the center of the circle. Work round and round in widening rings, sewing down the two gold strands together, and placing a couching stitch on each pencil line. Make sure no material shows between the rows of couching, yet do not crowd the rows so closely that they overlap one another. To end off with a smooth outline at the edge of the circle, plunge one gold thread through the fabric slightly ahead of the other.

Filling a Long Narrow Shape

When the shape to be filled is very thin and tapering, take only *one* of the pair of gold threads to the outer limit of the narrow shape at A) and sew it down with a double stitch for firmness at this point. Then double it on itself working it back to meet the second thread (at B). Turn *this* thread back sharply, stitching it with a double stitch, and continue them both together, as the shape widens, making a smooth flowing line as shown.

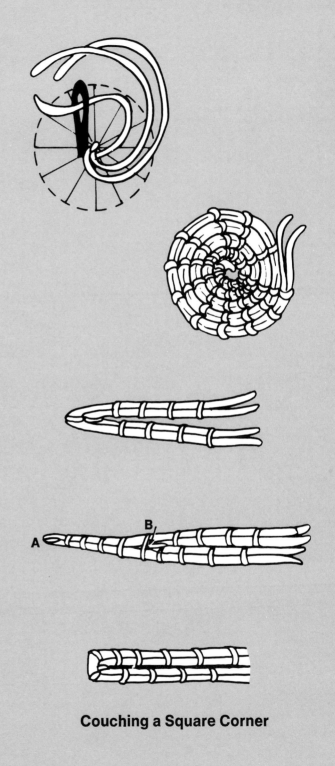

Couching a Square Corner

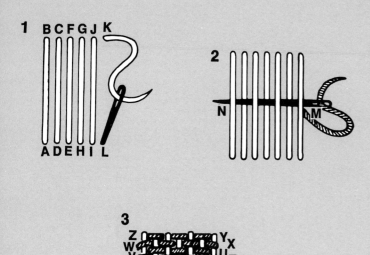

WEAVING STITCH

This is really exactly like sock darning! It may be done with at least two or three threads in both directions. Then when the weaving is completed evenly the result is a series of perfect squares in contrasting colors. It is also possible to use three or four threads for laying the first row of stitching, then to darn through with only one or two in the other direction. (This is useful to give a seeded effect on a strawberry, for instance.) Try to keep the outline even, for this stitch usually looks best if it is not outlined.

1. Come up at A, down at B, up at C, down at D, etc., laying threads side by side (the width of one thread apart).

2. Change to a blunt tapestry needle, and using a contrasting color, come up at M. Weave under and over the threads, starting through the center (or the widest part). Go down through the material at N.

3. Come up through the material at O, and weave through the threads, go down at P, up at Q, continue to Z, pushing threads together so that even squares of each color are obtained. Go back to the center (A), and finish weaving the lower part.

LAID WORK/Tied Diagonally

See also laid work on opposite page.

1. Having worked Laid Work over area (in direction shown), come up at A, down at B. This stitch lies across broadest area of the shape, to set the correct angle for the following stitches.

2. Come up at C, down at D, making a line parallel to A and B, about ¼″ above it. Then work from the center downwards until whole shape is laid with parallel slanting lines.

3. These lines must then be tied down with small stitches. Come up at A, down at B, going right through the material. These stitches should be placed alternately.

LAID WORK/Tied With Cross Bars

Laid Work may be used for large areas, since unlike satin stitch, no yarn is wasted on the reverse side. It may be held flat in many different ways by working other stitches on top in the opposite direction.

1. Needle comes up at A, goes in at B right across widest point of shape, to establish desired direction. All subsequent stitches are parallel to this line.

2. Next stitch comes up at C close to B and goes down again at D close to A. When Laid Work is done correctly, very small stitches appear on the reverse side, while the right side is closely covered with long threads.

3. Continue working in this way, coming up close beneath previous stitch, on the same side as where you went down. (Stitches should lie evenly side by side with no material showing between them.) When lower half is completed go back to center and work upper half in same way.

4. To hold Laid Work flat with Cross Bars, start in broadest part of shape and come up at A. Go down at B, laying a long thread diagonally across shape (angle is indicated by dotted line). This should cut across Laid Work threads at about 45°.

5. Come up at C, about ¼″ away from B, and go in at D, making a line parallel to A and B. Cover the whole shape in this way, and then work lines in the other direction to make perfect diamonds as shown in #6.

6. These threads are now tied down by a small stitch at each intersection. Come up at A, and go down at B, as shown, until all threads are tied down. At the edge make a little half stitch if necessary (as shown).

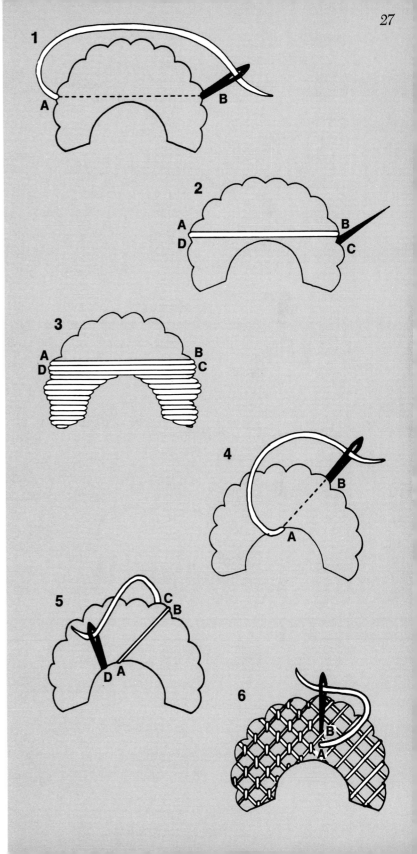

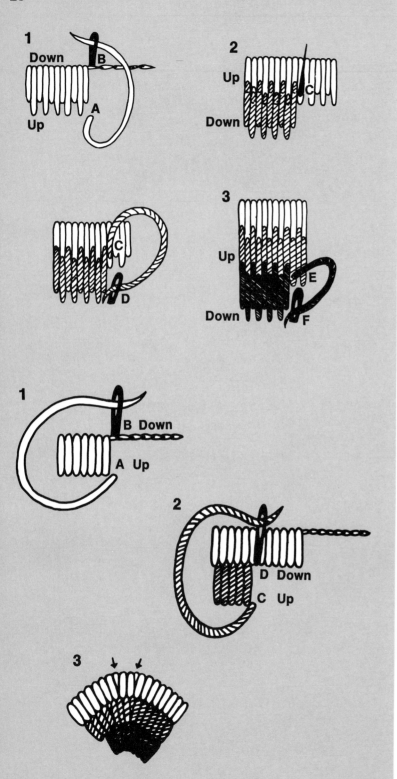

LONG AND SHORT STITCH/Tapestry Shading

Whole designs, including the background, may be worked in Tapestry Shading. The effect will be like its name; the vertical shading of tapestry. This is a good stitch to practice before trying Long and Short—Soft Shading, since you can experiment with the size of the stitch and correct blending of the colors without having to bother about changing direction. Use double thread for practicing so that the stitches are clear. Though the colors should blend, it is better to have a clearly defined difference between them to show the stitch to its best advantage. An outline afterwards will spoil the effect of the raised edge obtained by the Split Stitch padding.

BLOCK SHADING

Like Roumanian Stitch (see page 30), bands of Block Shading should fit closely together, slightly overlapping the previous row, to prevent any material showing between them. When used to fill shapes, Block Shading should have the same direction of stitch as Long and Short. It is advisable to mark this direction in pencil on the material before working. Never outline Block Shading afterwards, the edge will be smooth and raised because of the Split Stitch padding.

1. First outline shape to be worked with Split Stitch. Then work a row of Satin Stitches, bring needle up at A, down at B, over Split Stitch. (This makes a firm, even edge.) Keep all the stitches close and even, side by side.

2. Using the next shade, work a second row, repeating the first exactly. Come up at C, down at D, just between the stitches of the previous row. Block shading consists of even bands of Satin Stitches, changing color with each row, but showing a clear division between each band.

3. To work round a curve, place the stitches slightly wider apart on the edge, closer in the center to fan them, leaving no visible space between them, however. Occasionally slip in a shorter wedge stitch to help fan them (as shown in the diagram by the arrow).

LONG AND SHORT/Soft Shading

Long and Short—Soft Shading repeats the principle of Tapestry Shading exactly. Instead of running straight up and down, however, the stitches follow direction lines as indicated in the diagram.

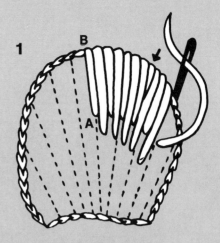

1. First draw guides in pencil on the material (as shown by dotted lines). Then outline the shape with Split Stitch, all around. Next work the first row of Long and Short, coming up at A and going down *over* the Split Stitch at B, starting in the center (or highest point) of each petal. It is easier to work downwards from the center on either side, since the angle of the stitch is straight to begin with, then gradually fans very slightly on each side. To achieve this, the stitches may be placed slightly wider apart on the outside edge and closer in the center, exactly like a fan. If this is not sufficient, a greater slant may be obtained by taking an extra short stitch over the upper edge occasionally (as indicated by the arrow in the diagram). This "wedge stitch" will not show, providing the next stitch is taken extremely close to it. On the shape illustrated, few wedge stitches are necessary since all the stitches gravitate to the center of the flower like the spokes of a wheel.

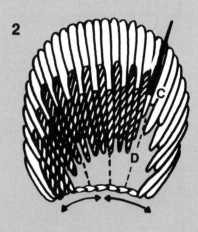

2. Work a second row of stitches in the next shade lighter or darker, coming up at C and down at D. Here again the stitches fan slightly as in the first row. They should not change direction abruptly, but should flow into one another smoothly. As in Tapestry Shading, be sure to split far enough back into the previous row and make the stitches long enough for the third row to split into them.

In the shape illustrated this second row of stitches comes right over the outline at the lowest point of the petals.

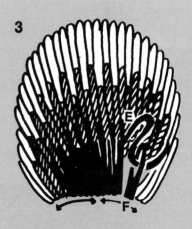

3. With the third color, fill the remaining space in the center of the petal. Come up at E and go down at F. Bring the stitches evenly down *over* the Split Stitch, making a smooth outline as at the beginning. On the third row it is impossible to fit each stitch *exactly* back through the previous stitch; every now and again miss one (as in the diagram). This is because there is less space in the center of the curve than on the outside. Still make the stitches look regular, keeping a long and short effect.

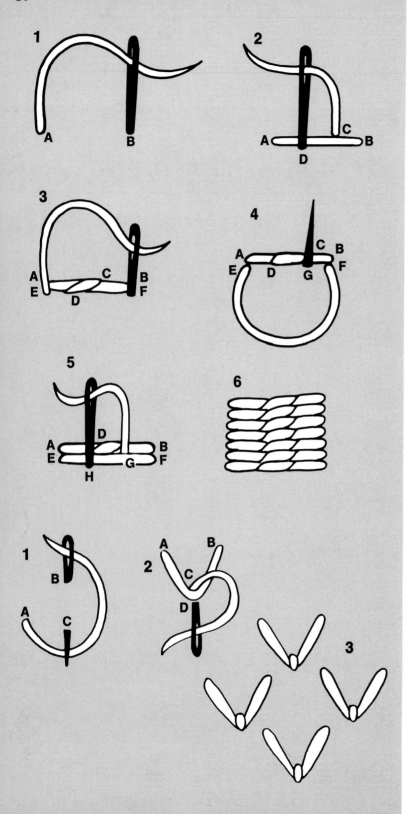

ROUMANIAN STITCH

Roumanian Stitch is really a straight Satin Stitch tied down with a smaller slanting stitch in the center. If the small stitch maintains its slant well, the stitches will fit closely together with no separation between them, keeping the effect smooth. However, this small stitch may be worked on a greater slant if the area to be filled is wide. When several bands are worked side by side the stitches should just overlap one another at the edge. If each row fits into the *exact* holes of the previous one, the stitches are apt to pull away a little and leave material showing in between.

1. Come up at A, down at B; pull flat.

2. Come up at C, and go over and down at D; pull flat.

3. Next, come up at E, below but touching A, go down at F, below but touching B; leave a loop.

4. Then come up at G, close to and immediately below C, inside the loop; draw tight.

5. Go down over thread at H, directly below D, exactly as in #2, and continue; repeating #3, 4, 5.

6. Keep center row of stitches G-H even (as shown in finished effect).

FLY STITCH

These stitches may be scattered over an area, or worked in regular rows. They are useful for holding flat other stitching such as laid work. In this case they may be worked right on top of the first layer of stitching.

1. Come up at A, go down at B, and come up at C. Loop the thread under the needle as shown and draw gently through.

2. Go down at D, over the loop to secure it.

3. Finished effect.

TURKEY WORK

Turkey Work is a series of loops cut to form a pile like a Turkey rug. For a different effect the loops may be left un-cut.

1. Go down at A, come up at B. Do not knot the thread, but leave about 1″ hanging on top (as shown in diagram #2). Arrow indicates direction of working.

2. With thread *below* the needle, on a line with A and B, go down at C, and come up in same hole as A. Draw this stitch tight, holding on to the loose end of thread (so that it does not pull right through the material).

3. With the thread *above* the needle, go down at D, come up in the same hole as C. *Do not* draw tight, but leave a loop (as shown). In this stitch, the needle should always be horizontal. (In order to show the stitch clearly in the diagram, it has been drawn on a slant.)

4. With the thread once more *below* the needle, go in at E, and up in the same hole as D; pull tight.

5. Continue along the line, coming up each time into the hole made by the previous stitch. The thread is alternately above the needle, leaving a loop, and below the needle drawing it tight.

6. Finished effect of single line. Work this stitch in lines one after the other. To achieve a thick velvety effect at the end, take small stitches and work the lines very close together. (This working diagram is much enlarged.)

7. Having filled the shape, cut all the loops along dotted line (as shown in diagram). Do not cut each line individually; trim the whole shape to the desired length (a full ⅛″ long).

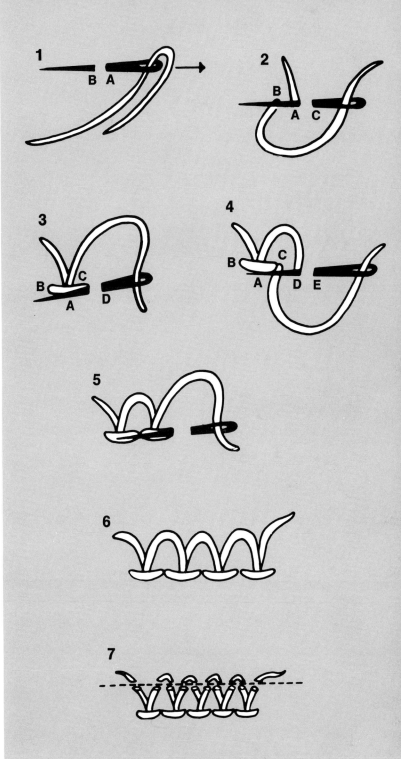

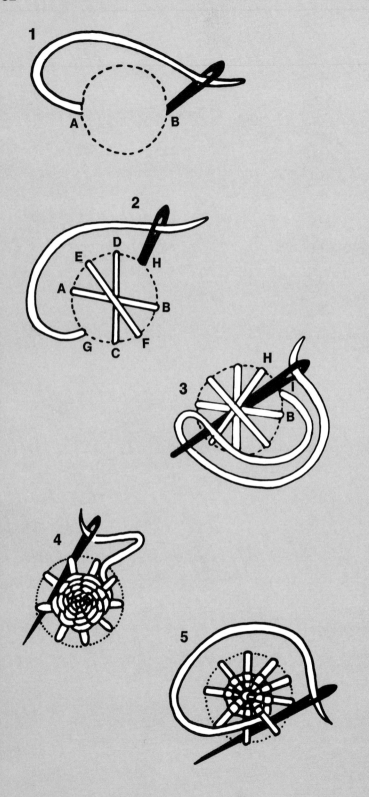

SPIDER'S WEB/Whipped/Woven

1. Using a blunt (tapestry) needle, come up at A, down at B, across center of circle.

2. Then come up at C, and down at D (C to D should be slightly off center as shown). Come up at E, down at F, up at G and down at H. (H goes in quite close to D.)

3. This leaves a space for the needle to come up finally at 1, a point midway between H and B. Then slide the needle under all the threads at their intersection. Take the thread and loop it across the needle and then under it as shown. Draw through and pull upwards to knot threads together in center.

Both Whipped and Woven Spider's Webs should be worked very tightly in the center to show the spokes clearly, loosening the threads slightly toward the outer edge. The spokes may be covered completely and the Spider's Web outlined or just the center may be worked, leaving the spokes showing all round. One or several colors may be used for each web, and one or more threads, depending on the size.

Woven

Starting in center, weave under and over spokes, round and round, till whole circle is filled. Outline circle with Stem Stitch or leave plain.

Whipped

With the same thread, starting in the center, slide under 2 threads. Then place needle behind the thread just taken, slide under it, plus a new one. Progress in this way, back one and under two, till the spokes are all covered. Then either outline circle with Stem Stitch or leave plain.

SHISHA STITCH

1. Place mylar circle in position and hold in place with two small stitches on either side (x). Then come up at A, close to edge of circle at left, and go down at B close to edge, to make a horizontal stitch one third down from top of circle. Come up at C, one third in from right of circle.

2. Continue around circle, from C to D, E to F, G to H, making a square as shown.

3. Repeat around circle, making four more stitches from I to J, K to L, M to N, O to P, to make a diamond on top of the square as shown. These are the "holding" stitches, which keep the circle firm.

4. Using a blunt needle, come up at A (anywhere close to left hand edge of circle). Slide needle under the "holding" threads, and with the thread under the needle draw tight.

5. Then take a little stitch into the fabric, close to the edge of the circle, from C to D. With thread looped under needle as shown, draw tight.

6. Repeat 4, sliding needle under the "holding" threads, and draw tight with the thread under the needle.

7. Repeat 5, but go down into the same hole, *inside* the loop at D. Come up at F with thread under needle. Continue, repeating steps 6 and 7 to make a close band of stitching around circle, catching in all the "holding" stitches so that they are completely concealed.

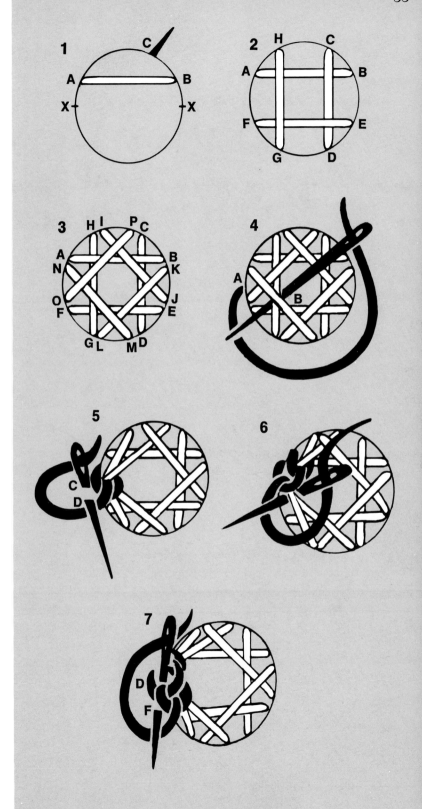

STITCHES IN STRIPES

OPPOSITE:

A pillow of striped ticking

A mirror frame of heavy wool fabric

OPPOSITE AND BELOW:

Boxes of plastic canvas—to fit tissue (square boxes) wool, or practically anything

All perfect for making samplers of stitches

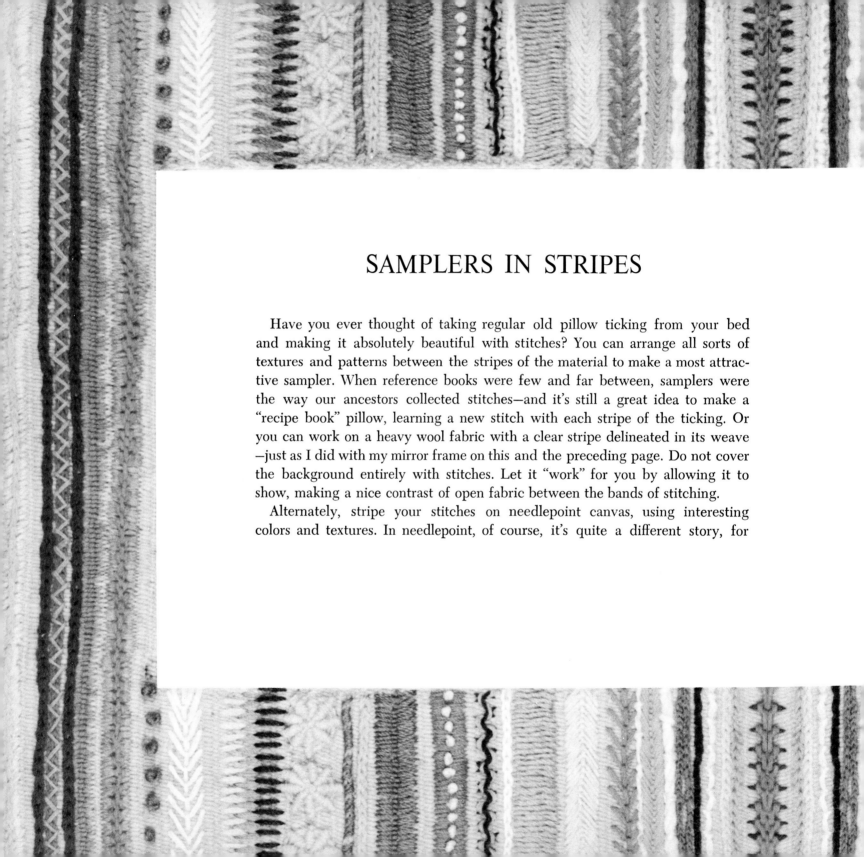

SAMPLERS IN STRIPES

Have you ever thought of taking regular old pillow ticking from your bed and making it absolutely beautiful with stitches? You can arrange all sorts of textures and patterns between the stripes of the material to make a most attractive sampler. When reference books were few and far between, samplers were the way our ancestors collected stitches—and it's still a great idea to make a "recipe book" pillow, learning a new stitch with each stripe of the ticking. Or you can work on a heavy wool fabric with a clear stripe delineated in its weave —just as I did with my mirror frame on this and the preceding page. Do not cover the background entirely with stitches. Let it "work" for you by allowing it to show, making a nice contrast of open fabric between the bands of stitching.

Alternately, stripe your stitches on needlepoint canvas, using interesting colors and textures. In needlepoint, of course, it's quite a different story, for you have to cover every inch of the background canvas—especially since in this case it's plastic! Plastic—or "space age canvas" (see page 91)—is a great new departure from the traditional cotton or linen needlepoint canvas because it is firm, yet flexible, needs no blocking, and can be cut to an exact size without fraying. As you can imagine, this makes it ideal for boxes, belts, coasters, handbags, or anything that needs to look tailored and professional when it's mounted. Before going shopping for materials (or turning out your bottom drawer!), turn to page 6 to find out which size needle to use with different yarns and fabrics. Pages 11 and 97 tell you how to begin and end off your thread, page 9 how to use a frame, and page 11 starts your library of crewel stitches. You will quickly learn that most of the crewel stitches are interchangeable—they can be worked as easily and effectively on needlepoint canvas as on linen, pillow ticking, or wool fabric.

You will find more detailed explanations of how to make both the mirror frame and boxes on pages 126 and 127.

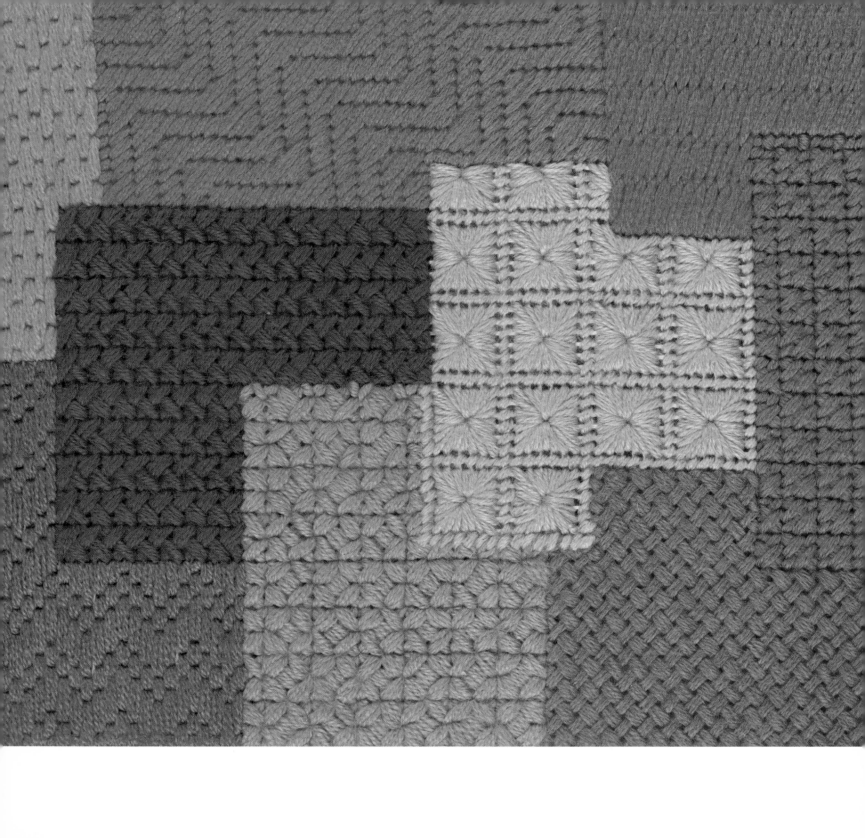

STITCHES IN NEEDLEPOINT
LEFT: Needlepoint stitch sampler
BELOW: Pansy "face" pillows in gobelin stitch

STITCHES IN NEEDLEPOINT

Beyond Tent Stitch—the regular needlepoint stitch —there are thousands of fancy stitches for you to play with. Here is just a small sampling to whet your appetite, but there are literally hundreds of lovely textures, with names as romantic as they are intriguing to work. Gobelin, which takes its name from the famous tapestry weaving establishment in France; Byzantine; Oriental; Algerian Eyelets; Web Stitch— you can combine them in a design, add them as extra texture to an otherwise flat needlepoint, like the frosting on a cake, or use any one of them to do an entire design, like the pansy pillows on the previous pages. These were done in Encroaching Gobelin, a stitch that gives a smooth, interlocked effect of woven tapestry.

Your sampler can be made of geometric shapes— the recipe for working it, together with your library of needlepoint stitches, starts on page 97. The three pansy pillows I worked are shown on pages 128–131, but you could plant a whole "garden" of flower faces —no two alike, stitched with the marvelous color combinations nature can inspire.

1. Chevron
2. Long-Armed Cross Stitch
3. Brick Stitch
4. Rice Stitch
5 Algerian Eyelet with Tent Stitch
6. Oriental Stitch
7. Web Stitch
8. Rice Stitch Variation
9. Encroaching Gobelin
10. Step Stitch
11. Brick Stitch—Long and Short Variation

CHRISTMAS TREE

Everybody has those boxes of Christmas decorations that they put away every year, and what fun it is to open them up just before Christmas and rediscover all the things that have been saved since childhood. I thought it would be nice to make a Christmas tree in crewel which you could bring out every year. Who knows, it might even become an heirloom, with your grandchildren still treasuring it years later! The tree has the effect of ribbons wrapped around a base of snowy white linen. The foundation is a styrofoam cone—you can buy many different sizes from the florist or variety store. To make the tree, follow the pattern and instructions on page 132, working the pine needles with long, straight dark-green stitches that make a perfect background for your "decorations" of Bullion Knots, Padded Satin, and Spiders' Webs. I wanted to keep my trees very "crewelly," because I felt the velvet effect of crewel wool would contrast well with all the other tinsel decorations at Christmas. But you could experiment with brilliant cottons, metal threads, or even jewels. For a completely different effect you could work the textured stitches on a background of needlepoint canvas, if you prefer.

CHRISTMAS TREE
OPPOSITE:
Crewel stitches mounted on a styrofoam cone

GRAPHICS FROM A TO Z
Flowers of satin stitch in wool and cotton

GRAPHICS FROM A TO Z

Graphics: initials, monograms—you can have an alphabet of designs for embroidery right at your fingertips. The letters make such good patterns by themselves, but more than that, they give a personal touch to your needlework, which is the essence of making something yourself. It's just for *you*, or the special friend for whom you made it.

For a dramatic effect—super graphics!—you could try my flowering letters shown here and on the previous page. The turnback of a sheet or a pillowcase with his and her initials is a great idea for a wedding present, but a shirt, a sweater, or a handbag would be equally effective. For your instructions on how to go about the whole thing, turn to page 135.

GEOMETRIC NEEDLEPOINT

Stone carvings, mosaics, and peasant costumes are inspirations for all kinds of marvelous geometric designs, both simple and intricate. Needlepoint canvas is the perfect background for them because of its regular square mesh, which is so easy to count.

Start with the simplest form—criss-cross lines making diamonds, which you can fill in with a patchwork of different colors. You can use up your leftover wools, because your harlequin pattern can grow happily as you go along.

You begin by working a double row of Tent stitches (shown below) across the entire canvas in either direction, to form diamonds. Work these in either a very light or very dark shade to form a strong contrast with the colors you are going to use later. Then fill each diamond with a different color to make the harlequin pattern. You can fill in with flat colors like the tasseled pillow here or shade each diamond like the little pincushion on the next page, which was done with brilliant jewel-like colors.

The whole effect becomes different in finer scale, or if you fill in the diamonds with another stitch—such as the bolster with Algerian Eyelets. You could work all in Bargello (the upright bolster) or try a lovely fancy stitch that gives a three-dimensional basket effect as in the workbag, in blue and yellow on the next page.

GEOMETRIC NEEDLEPOINT

Geometric patterns also can be worked out in any of the textures from your sampler of needlepoint stitches. The shoulder bag, for instance, shown on page 119, and in color on page 47, is done in Gobelin Stitch. The simpler the stitch, the more intense the color, because there are no twists or braids to break up the light. The tennis racket cover is dramatic in its effect, for the same reason. It is also Gobelin Stitch, as is the very simple handbag I made for myself with my initials back to back, forming a geometric pattern. Begin all geometric patterns in the center of the space to be covered, so that they will be balanced and equal on all four sides. Especially if the area is small, you will find it easier to establish your pattern by working the center first, then filling in the half stitches around the edges later. You will find patterns for all the designs starting on page 114 and you can use them in all sorts of different and exciting ways. Don't begin unless you can spare the time—you won't be able to put them down!

DESIGNING NEEDLEPOINT

Transferring a design for needlepoint is the easiest thing in the world. If you can trace, you can put a design onto needlepoint canvas, because the canvas is transparent and you can just lay your design underneath and trace it through. Since you are going to cover the whole canvas with close stitches, if you do make a mistake in tracing it won't matter too much, because your light outlines are all going to be covered up! But you must use a fine-tipped permanent marking pen. If it isn't waterproof, when you finally block your beautiful finished design the ink might run into your wool, which would be disastrous.

First of all, you must have a design, and this may be influenced by where you want to use your finished tapestry. The combination of tough canvas and close stitches makes needlepoint the best wearing form of embroidery, so it is ideal for rugs, chair seats, belts, and handbags, as well as pillows or pictures. I needed a pillow in our library, so what could be better than using the library curtains—one of my favorite designs from Jack Lenor Larsen—as the basis for my design? The photos show how you go about transferring it to canvas.

First lay a piece of acetate (heavy transparent film) over the textile, tape it in position and with a *permanent* marker (nothing else will stay on the acetate) trace the main outlines of the design. The next step is to lay some tracing paper under the acetate (to make the black lines very clear), and tape the canvas flat on top. Make sure that (1) the selvedge runs up and down vertically, for better wear; (2) the canvas is square and runs parallel with your straight lines around your design; and (3) you leave at least a 4″ margin all around. You can always cut off extra canvas but you can't add! Finally, trace the pattern on to the canvas with the same permanent marker. If you cut your canvas on the floor as I often do, the cat will enjoy helping with the project!

Now you can do one of two things. Either fill the colors by painting the canvas with oil paint or work directly on the plain outlined canvas with wool, keeping the original pattern beside you to follow for color placement. I prefer the second method because you keep your design complete for constant checking as you go along. When you work over a painted canvas you can't compare the final result with your original design.

There's a third method, which is to follow a graph in counting each stitch out on the canvas. A graph is a "must" for geometric designs such as the tassled border for the stool on the next page, because the pattern has to be repeated exactly. But you can also reproduce a "free" design exactly in this way. The graph for the pillow design plus helpful general hints to help you start are on page 136.

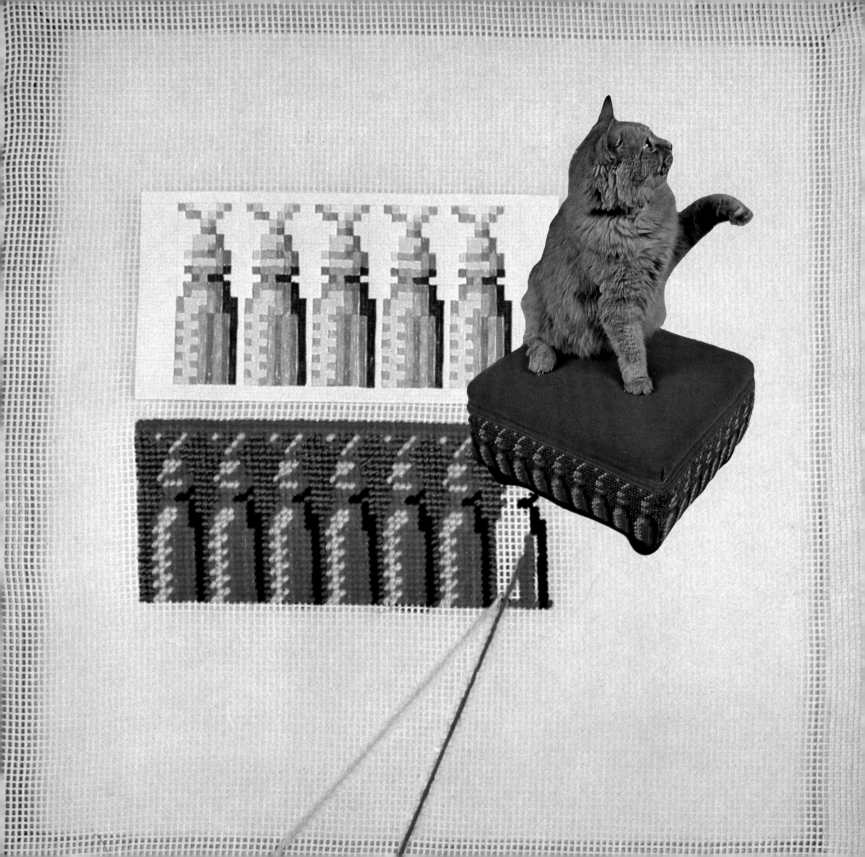

OPPOSITE:

BELL PULLS, BORDERS AND BANDINGS
Footstool with a tassel border counted out on canvas
from a graph

DESIGNING NEEDLEPOINT
Curtains in a library used as an inspiration for a
needlepoint pillow

BORDERS, BANDINGS, AND BELL PULLS

Border designs are so effective because you can add subtle touches of embroidery to enrich a large area such as curtains or a bedspread. Bandings for the border of a stool, luggage-rack straps, belts, hat bands, guitar straps, curtain tiebacks, or valances can all be most decorative, and the everlasting bell pull (which certainly has outlived its original use, since there is no one to answer if you pull!) makes a most unusual wall panel—its narrow size is often just right for certain areas. I asked my daughter, Jessica, to make a hat band to illustrate this chapter —and guess what she came up with: a whole hat! She bought a plain felt hat and said she wanted to embroider it as though she had picked flowers and pushed them under the band, or as though they were growing all over the brim and cascading down from it. So I taught her to make pompoms—which *my* mother had taught me—and she made them in bright yellow, pink, and green to contrast with the coral blossoms on the hat.

My friend, Gay deMenocal, made six pairs of curtains that I designed for her. Part of one of the borders is shown on this page. It was not as long a prospect as you might suppose. The narrow bandings and the fact that every section was varied with different stitches and color made the work much faster. (Gay might not have had quite the same story to tell if you were to ask her!) But I think only exact repeats seem endless— as long as you have a change of pace everything grows rapidly. The design and the stitches Gay used are shown on pages 138 and 139.

Borders and bandings in needlepoint are as effective as crewel, because you can apply a band of tapestrylike needlepoint to velvet or similar fabric with very rich and lovely results. The stool banding on page 50 is a case in point. The tassels have an effect of *trompe l'oeil* because a few very dark stitches form the deep shadow on one side and a few very light stitches highlight the opposite side of each tassel. The pattern can be counted out stitch by stitch from the graph shown on the same page.

I worked in tent stitch on #7 canvas with Persian rug wool, but if you prefer you could work in Cross Stitch on finer canvas to give each stitch a stylized square effect, rather like mosaic.

TO MAKE POMPOMS

Cut two cardboard disks (shirt cardboard is good) with holes in the center as shown, place them together and wrap with wool by rolling lengths into a small enough ball to pass through the hole. When sufficient wrapping closes the hole, slip points of scissors between disks; clip wool all around outer edge. Draw a strand of yarn between the disks, wrap several times around, secure with a double knot, leaving ends long for attaching pompom. Tear away disks and trim evenly.

DESIGNS FROM CHINA

OPPOSITE: Willow Pattern in crewel

ABOVE: Chinese apple blossoms in cross stitch

DESIGNS FROM CHINA

No, we're not necessarily rushing off to the Orient here—just to the china closet! The ideas on a willow pattern plate for instance—how fabulous they can be in crewel. Or an Italian majolica plate: colors, simplicity of design all ready waiting for stitches—unequalled inspiration! Willow pattern china has always been a favorite of mine—blue houses, blue people, blue trees, with all the possibilities of texture such as Fishbone Stitch willows and French Knot pines. The willow-pattern design is shown on page 142. You could work it either in shades of pale and deep blue on white linen, or in blue and white on sky-blue denim as I did on page 54.

Simple blue and white is always so effective, and the Chinese apple-blossom bowl was the inspiration for the Cross Stitch table mat on the opposite page. The pattern for the mat is on page 141. You could use any of your favorite china as inspiration for a Cross Stitch pattern or you could take an old design and make it quite contemporary by enlarging its scale, such as my Napoleon plate on this page. Big straight stitches in bold yellow radiating from one central hole make the effective flowers on a white linen pillow with huge blue French Knots in between.

The Delft monkey with its patterned tail was yet another idea for a bedspread in yellow-striped velvet. Instead of filling the design solidly with stitches, I decided to let the fabric of the background shine through in contrast to the close blue stitching of the body.

Don't forget needlepoint, of course! Miniature flowers, bees, and bugs from eighteenth-century Chelsea china plates would make a lovely set of dining-room chairs, but I could go on for ever . . . I'd better stop and let you start stitching!

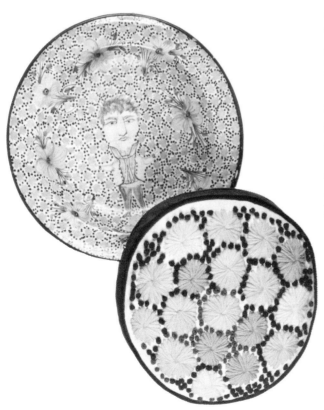

BARGELLO

Bargello—how on earth did it get such a strange name? This beautiful soft shading worked on canvas was done in Florence in the sixteenth century and a rather intriguing story grew up about it. Five chairs, worked in shades of green and gold, still stand in the Bargello palace in Florence, and it was thought that prisoners were taught to do this form of needlework while they were held in the jail. However, that seems implausible when you learn that they were taken there only when they were about to be condemned to death. It is doubtful that their final hours would have been spent doing such peaceful stitching, soothing as it may be to the mind!

You may hear of it referred to as Hungarian Point, Florentine Stitch, or Flame Stitch, but Bargello does seem to be the most romantic name for these rainbows of smooth stitches. Beautiful colors, the blending of subtle shades or the contrasting of brilliant ones, makes Bargello as fascinating to work as it is exciting to the eye.

In order to show the stitches clearly on television, I worked in bold rug wool, and then discovered that the large scale was most effective and contemporary even when used for something as traditional as a Queen Anne piano bench. The pattern is the green and olive one shown on the next page, and you see how the shading can give a wonderfully three-dimensional effect. Our hall sofa was done in finer scale on number-ten canvas, because I wanted the effect of watered silk. Worked in yellow and white with a touch of gray, the design is shown below and on the next page. The boots, chair seat, and curtain tieback were all done with the same pattern in magenta, lavender, and orange. Thus you can see how versatile Bargello can be. By simply changing the scale, a stitch here or there, or the colors (perhaps even by making a mistake!), you can develop your own original design.

You will find all the patterns shown here on pages 124 and 125.

BARGELLO

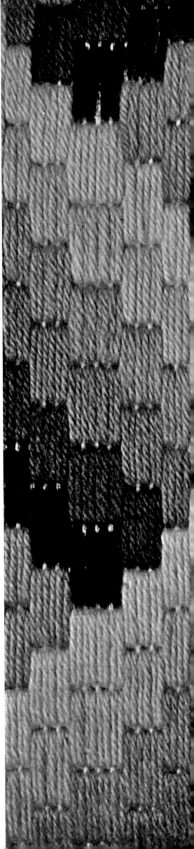

ROUMANIAN STITCH

Roumanian Stitch, of course, must have come from Roumania, otherwise how would it have gotten its name? Although it was used in all the Balkan countries on all kinds of peasant costumes, when I learned how to do it at the Royal School of Needlework in England, I learned it under a group of stitches called Oriental Laidwork, which makes me think that like a lot of other stitches it probably originated in China. At any rate, the early American settlers just adored this stitch and they used it in preference to Long and Short (the usual shading stitch used for crewel embroidery in England). You see Roumanian Stitch is really a sort of Satin Stitch with a little stitch that just holds it flat in the center. So you can do Long stitches, hold each one down securely and make bands of this stitching, blending each band smoothly into the previous one, giving a textured, yet shaded, effect. I think that the New England settlers probably liked Roumanian because they could save their yarn. On the back of the work, it leaves practically nothing at all . . . just two little stitches. This is probably why it was sometimes called New England Economy Stitch! When the busy housewife had to start with a sheep, and clean, spin, and dye her own wool, she certainly wasn't going to waste it on the wrong side of her embroidery. So it really did seem to be the perfect solution. On this page, I covered a box with a very New England pattern—all in Roumanian with a few French Knots. On page 63 are another peaceful pastoral landscape of the sort our New England ancestors loved to depict on their petticoat borders and also a spring tapestry of snowdrops and winter aconites. You can see how you can make the bands of stitching curve and flow in smooth lines. And you can compare it with the Satin Stitch on the same page and see what a textured look Rumanian has—excellent for hills and groundings. The patterns for the two tapestries are on pages 144 and 146.

SATIN STITCH

I'm wearing my great-grandmother's dress, which came from the Paris exhibition of 1851. (She had an eighteen-inch waist, which I had to modify *considerably* in order to fit into it!) But the whole dress of antique gold is beautifully stitched with red roses and blue forget-me-nots in Satin Stitch.

Satin Stitch is called by that name for a very simple reason—it looks like satin! Whether it's done in silk or wool the stitches are so close together they have a marvelous satiny effect, and the flowers on this dress are really the epitome of it because they are so padded and shiny. When I made my Satin Stitch sampler of blue poppies (you will see it when you turn to the next page), I worked ing rug wool to show the angle of each stitch clearly. There's a trade secret to getting the edges of the petals even. You first *split*-stitch them all around, then work right *over* the split-stitch edge (see page 18). This forms a padding, which helps to keep your outlines. No one knows it's there—it's your secret.

The morning glories on the trellis are also done in Satin Stitch, but on needlepoint canvas. The background is shaded with long and short Satin and the canvas is entirely covered. I love the look of this straight stitching on canvas and it's so quick and easy. I call these designs "Crewel Point Tapestries," and you'll find more on the pages that follow. For patterns and instructions, turn to pages 148–152.

SATIN STITCH

Satin stitch used in crewel (OPPOSITE)
and in needlepoint (ABOVE)

ROUMANIAN STITCH

RIGHT: Roumanian stitch used for hills and
as an overall tapestry

GARDEN OF EDEN SATIN STITCH

Forget for a moment the tiny time-consuming Tent stitches of regular needlepoint, and try making a crewel-point tapestry. You will be amazed at the ease and speed with which you can finish a design and the effectiveness of colorful long Satin stitches.

Satin Stitch, a little Stem Stitch, and a few French Knots are the basic stitches for this quick and effective way of making a wall hanging, a tabletop under glass, or a mirror frame. Work the stitches either straight up and down vertically, or across horizontally. Fill each area, working from one side of the shape to the other, placing the stitches side by side. If the area is too large it may have to be divided by making 2 shorter stitches. But since these tapestries are mainly to be used as wall hangings, the stitches will not be pulled or caught when its design is in use, so they can be left fairly long without danger.

Leave the background *open* in contrast to the smooth, flat stitching of the design, or fill it with "Random Bargello" (long and short stitches), as I did in the two pillows on this page. Where necessary, add texture such as French Knots or Turkey Work and outlines in Stem or Back Stitch.

The patterns and instructions are on pages 150 and 151.

TURKEY WORK

This marvelous, strokable, velvety stitch is perfect for all sorts of animals, bugs, and the centers of daisies . . . not to mention bees and bull rushes (cat-tails to you!). It has its origins in tufted Oriental rugs (that's how it got its name), but the main thing about it is its mystery. Everybody thinks it's just about impossible to do—it looks so difficult. But really, it isn't.

If you take a gigantic piece of wool and a dagger of a needle and start stitching, you'll see that in principal it's really very simple. Once you have followed the step-by-step instructions on page 154 and learned how, you can decide whether you want a looped or tufted effect, and either trim it or leave it uncut. For a really silky effect you can go one step further and work each of the stitches spaced slightly apart, then cut them and brush them with a teasing brush or comb. I call this simply "Brushed Wool" Stitch and it's a useful trick to know if you've done Turkey Work accidently and left a few bald spots in the middle. Just brush it out and fluff it a little and no one will know!

SENTIMENTS IN STITCHES

This was done by Mary Pitt
Who hated every stitch of it!

Our great-grandmother's samplers are so expressive . . . all the more so because they were stitched. One can imagine the young girl of tender age painstakingly counting out "Youth is the season for improvement" in Cross Stitch on her linen.

But there *is* something about stitching a saying or a poem that seems to give the message greater significance, and one of the inspiring things about samplers is the way pattern and words were integrated. My husband, Vladimir, designed this pillow—which says "Love" and "Peace" at the same time—and I worked it in red and blue Chain Stitch on white velvet, but I think it would equally be magnificent in needlepoint, perhaps with textured stitches.

I always loved Shakespeare's poems to spring and winter from *Love's Labour's Lost*:

> *When Daisies pied and Violets blue*
> *and Lady Smocks all Silver White*
> *and Cuckoo Buds of Yellow hue*
> *do paint the meadows with delight . . .*

and

> *When icicles hang by the wall*
> *and Dick the Shepherd blows his nail*
> *and Tom bears logs into the hall*
> *and milk comes frozen home in pail . . .*

I designed the two pictures on the next page to illustrate the poems with the words forming a frame around them. Back Stitch is the most useful stitch for this—in fact, it's ideal for all lettering, even if you want to sign your finished masterpiece. If you turn to page 155 you will find instructions for an easy way to put all sorts of sentiments, verses, or your signature onto the material, together with the patterns for Shakespeare's songs to spring and winter.

OVERLEAF:
SENTIMENTS IN STITCHES
Shakespeare's Songs to Winter and
Spring illustrated in crewel.

THINKING BIG

Make a crewel covering for an antique armchair! It's a grand project that absolutely shows your expertise and is so much more lasting and inspiring than an eyeglass case or a coaster. I chose an overall pattern, because even if a leaf or stem doesn't quite fit, the design is intended to grow all over and it won't matter in the least if a small bit gets cut off.

To make your design, first cut a pattern in muslin to fit your chair. I like to sketch the general outline of the design right on the muslin with a felt marker. You can fill in the details later, as you see by the finished closeup of the pattern on the previous page. It's such a help to visualize your finished design right on the chair, and to get the main outlines balanced first. If you draw an eighteenth-century design of flowing stems and flowers, make sure that the stems always grow, never fall off backward, where they join the main stem.

Use a tough, hard-wearing background fabric, or quilt the background after you have finished the crewel, for a really rich effect. Fine wools combined with silk or cotton can sometimes be longer-lasting and harder-wearing than big bold ones, because the stitches are smaller and closer. For the details of how to transfer the design and do the embroidery, turn to page 160.

OVERLEAF:
THINKING BIG
Queen Anne armchair in fine crewel wools in linen twill.

SCATTERED BLOSSOMS

Have you ever wanted to do crewel embroidery, yet not quite felt up to designing your own? Well, here's a great idea. Simply go out and buy damasks, brocaded fabrics, or printed linen, and *re-embroider* the scattered blossom designs on the material, adding your own color to the already patterned background.

Just like working on pillow ticking, this is a way of stitching without even having to transfer your design to fabric, much less having to draw it first, because your pattern is already there. You could do dining-room chairs with a touch of color added to the brocade background, or make pillows with an eighteenth-century pattern of roses as I did on the next page. Just follow the pattern, edging it with Long and Short stitches—adding criss-cross patterns or a sprinkling of French Knots in deeper shades than the background. Or choose a printed linen like the pineapples on page 73, work just one of the pineapples, and use it as a pillow on a sofa covered with the same fabric. You can cover the design with Satin and Long and Short stitches. Don't do *too* much stitching though—allow the material to show through so that the design looks light. You are just adding color and texture where you need it.

As you see, the idea can be traditional or contemporary. My husband, who is a modern-furniture designer, made me the rocking chair that is shown on the next page, so I chose a softly printed linen fabric and scattered my own blossoms on it, letting them fade off on the seat to show only the plain fabric. The bold stitches on the printed linen give a very nice three-dimensional effect. The headboard of a bed, curtains, valances, pillows, chair seats, or stool tops are just a few of the many things you could imagine enriched by this technique.

SCATTERED BLOSSOMS

Re-embroidered fabrics with designs inspired by the
background material
OPPOSITE: Printed linen on contemporary Vladimir
Kagan rocking chair
RIGHT: Scalamandre silk pillows and Arthur H. Lee
pineapple design linen

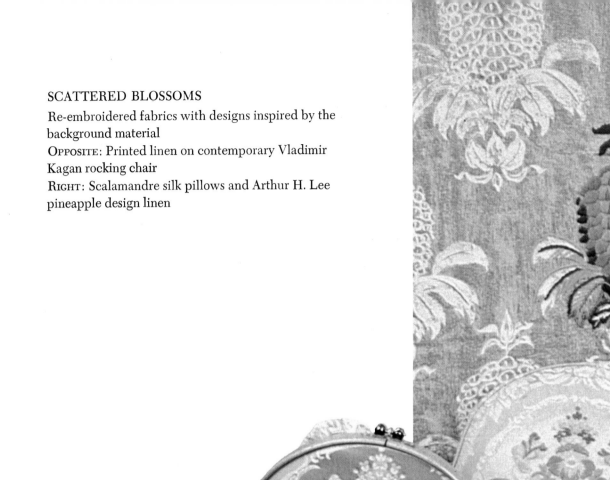

STORIES IN STITCHES

Somebody once said "We're all tall children," and perhaps that's why I still love the illustrations from children's books so much, particularly the ones I grew up with. You can say the naive simplicity and direct approach are just perfect for stitchery, but it's more than that—there's an aura, a mood that every creature from the world of make-believe communicates to us. My younger daughter, Vanessa, and son, Illya, are looking at their favorite of the little books by Beatrix Potter (if they *have* only one favorite, which I doubt!), and some of the embroideries I worked from them are shown on the next pages.

Hunca Munca, the mouse who invaded the doll house, and rocked her babies to sleep in the doll cradle, is done in crewel point, with her babies nearly buried under a lovely thick blanket of uncut Turkey Work. 'Grandma" mouse is knitting a very realistic sock done in Raised Stem Stitch, and other friends, such as Peter Rabbit and Squirrel Nutkin, are welcoming a newborn baby into the world on the birth sampler. (The design also makes an excellent mirror or photo frame.)

Look through *your* favorites for inspiration and have the drawings photostatically enlarged or reduced to the size you need. It's a mistake to try to include too much—abstract the character from its background and your needlework will have more impact. Then comes the fun part, choosing color and stitch that will best tell the story for you. Imagine Winnie the Pooh in furry Turkey Work floating down under a balloon of Padded Satin Stitch in shiny cotton, Toad from *The Wind in the Willows*, very "toady" green in his textured wicker chair, or Peanuts sleeping on top of the dog house in bold needlepoint with brilliant colors. Take your choice, and if you would like to experiment with the designs shown on the next page, turn to pages 162-165.

CREWEL POINT

Opposite:
STORIES IN STITCHES

CREWEL POINT

Crewel point . . . that marvelous combination of stitches on canvas that gives you such a rich textured effect and that can broaden your whole thinking about the possibilities of needlepoint.

There are two ways of going about it. Either add the crewel stitches as three-dimensional accent like the frosting on the cake, as I did in the designs on this and the opposite page, or use crewel stitches *exclusively* to cover the canvas like the clogs at the left, the boxes on page 34 or the Satin Stitch morning glories on page 63, or the Garden of Eden on page 65. In either case, you can use the regular canvas mesh to keep your stitches even when you need to count them, while at other times you treat the canvas as though it were embroidery linen. In this case you work right over the canvas freely, just as you would if you were doing crewel stitching on linen—its usual background fabric. The split-stitched ribbon on the top of the basket opposite illustrates this, or the padded Satin Stitch flowers and grapes in the same design.

Hunca Munca on the previous page (and on page 165) was done with the blanket over the cradle in the raised loops of Turkey Work, and the baby's dress in angora Chain Stitch. This is the fun of crewel point, choosing stitches that perfectly represent the spirit of what you are trying to capture—they tell the story for you.

You will find the possibilities endless and the combinations almost unlimited. Have fun, but don't get too carried away. Be selective, eliminating too many colors and stitches in case the overall effect becomes cluttered. A repeated stitch here or there often can be more restful.

THINKING BIGGER
Designs in bold scale
using rug wools combined
with crewel yarns

THINKING BIGGER

Marvelous heavy wools and textured fabrics can give you a whole new dimension, because traditional embroidery stitches look completely contemporary when they're in huge scale. You can make a wall hanging or a room divider with all the qualities of a tapestry, except that it won't take you nearly as long, because you'll be using rug wools on bold-weave fabric with large, open areas of background.

This owl shows what you can do with the large scale—the great breakthrough here is getting the design onto the material. Transferring a pattern to nubbly fabric sometimes can seem next to impossible—these illustrations show you how to go about it easily. First, trace or draw your design on paper. Next, lay a piece of net, lawn, tulle, or crinoline over the drawing, and tape it down to prevent it from slipping. With a broad-tipped marking pen, trace your design onto the net. Now lay the net on top of the material and tape it down in the correct position. Once more outline your design with the broad-tipped pen. You will find that the marker penetrates the net and shows through on your fabric quite clearly.

If your background fabric is dark, you may have to just touch it up wherever necessary after you remove the net to make any faint lines more definite. If your background fabric is light, make sure you test first to see that your felt-tipped marker is not too broad and your lines do not run through too heavily. For instructions on stitching the owl shown here and on the previous page, turn to page 167.

NEEDLEPAINTING

Have you ever realized that you could paint a picture with needles and thread that's every bit as exciting, varied, and unlimited as an oil or a watercolor, and certainly twice as portable? There's a tradition for painting with a needle. In the eighteenth century beautiful pictures were made in silk thread on a silk background. These were usually very fine with tiny flat stitches, sometimes with part of the design painted as well as stitched. In complete contrast is Van Gogh's "Apple Orchard" on the next page. The impressionist painters give us such an opportunity for texture and dimension in stitches.

Start by mounting your design on an artists' stretcher frame (as in the photos), slightly larger than your finished picture to allow you to work up to the edges. Use a power stapler, start in the center of each side and work out to the corners, stretching the fabric tightly and keeping the threads straight. Do your stitching in layers; first the long white straight stitches in the sky, then the little trees in the distance, then the large tree trunks in the foreground, then the ground itself, and finally the apple blossoms. These are done with raised, loose stitches—which really gives the effect of impasto oil painting.

It's a great experience to interpret someone else's painting into stitches. You can learn by it, so you will be bold enough to make your own—and that's the most enjoyable of all. For more details about the Van Gogh shown here, turn to page 168.

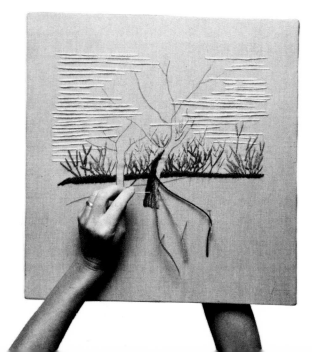

OVERLEAF:
NEEDLEPAINTING
Van Gogh's Apple Orchard adapted for crewel.

CROSS STITCH

On the preceding page my daughter, Jessica, aged sixteen, is wearing the Cross Stitch blouse I made for her. At the age of three she persuaded me to give her a needle and thread and an embroidery hoop, so she could stitch "just like Mommy." Like most children being taught by their "mums," she said, "Go away, I can do it better all on my own!" And the first real stitch she did all on her own was a Cross Stitch . . . which really shows what an absolutely fascinating primitive stitch it is. If you do it a little more neatly than Jessica's first efforts, you must work on an even-weave fabric, or on needlepoint canvas, so that you can count the threads to keep your stitches even. Some of the earliest Cross Stitch embroideries came from the Greek islands, where really beautiful peasant blouses were made, but not all of us have time for those very fine stitches. Lawn or organza fabric with a weave that suggests a mesh or grid is perfect, because it allows you to make a bold pattern, fitting each Cross Stitch into the square of the fabric, so your peasant blouse won't take you a lifetime! There are lots of similar materials—checked gingham, for instance. I monogrammed a shirt for Jessica in red, on blue-and-white-checked gingham, with a cross covering each square. The pattern for the peasant blouse is on page 170, the letters for monogramming are on page 171, and you will find your lesson in Cross Stitch on page 20.

OVERLEAF:
CROSS STITCH
Jessica wearing her cross stitched peasant blouse.

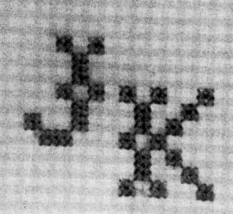

APPLIQUE

Appliqué is a French word for the simplest form of stitching in the world, sewing one piece of fabric on top of another—in other words, "applied" work. Start with the very simplest—make a felt oven mitt, cutting out circles in brilliant colors, one smaller than the other, and hold them in place with a single fat French Knot. You can buy a quilted mitt from the five-and-ten and just dress it up by slipping your embroidered one over it.

Another fascinating form of appliqué is combined with patchwork. The crazy quilt shown on page 89 was made in the 1800s, with all kinds of embroidered and printed patches appliquéd to a backing with Feather Stitch. Sometimes these were made in the form of friendship quilts. Each person contributed her special motif or signature, which really makes a lovely heirloom.

You could sew ribbons to a backing to make a magnificent skirt like the one I'm wearing on the next page, which was made for me by Nantucket Looms. The purple pillow on the same page was done with simple velvet ribbons, just machine-stitched down to the background of cotton fabric. Beside them in the chair are pillows made of long strips of material, cut and joined to form a diamond pattern. The instructions for the pillows are on page 174.

Reverse appliqué is a little more involved, but so effective. The San Blas Indians of Panama are great exponents of the idea. The skirt on page 90 shows their work—brilliant colors, with an almost heraldic effect. Below the skirt is a felt table mat I made with reverse appliqué—the instructions for it are on page 172.

APPLIQUE
LEFT: Skirt and pillows appliquéd with ribbons
OPPOSITE: Heirloom crazy quilt, pieced with silk ribbons, velvets and satins, embroidered in silk and chenille

REVERSE APPLIQUE
Skirt made from "Molas" from the San Blas Indians.
Table mat of appliquéd felt.

SPACE AGE CANVAS

Needlepoint canvas has evolved through the years from its humble origin of plain soft-woven textile to its present-day form of stiffened mesh —which is so easy to work on. Now science has added a new dimension—plastic canvas! It's a great asset to the modern needleworker for many projects that need mounting, such as belts, handbags, coasters, eyeglass cases, boxes—in fact everything that has to be firm yet flexible is ideal for plastic canvas. I made a handbag in the shape of our Nantucket house. You could make your own, and if you get ambitious you could stitch the family looking out of the windows—or at any rate the dog or cat! The principle is exactly the same as the little houses that were designed to hang on the Christmas tree, perhaps with a tiny light inside to shine through the windows, or you could make a whole village and use it as a centerpiece on the table.

The little baskets make pincushions or work boxes, or may be filled with candies and hung on the tree. The work-box version with a padded, frilled pincushion on top could be embroidered with your or a friend's initials—it makes a perfect gift. (All these are shown in color on the next page.)

Plastic canvas needs no blocking, and your finished piece can be joined to the next without turn-ing backs or stiffening, so your finished results will be tailored and professional-looking. So far, plastic canvas is available only in sheets, size 13½" x 10½", but as of this writing, Du Pont is experimenting with all sizes of mesh and in the same widths as regular canvas. Instructions for making the baskets and houses are on page 174–177.

SPACE AGE CANVAS
Flower basket pincushions.
Basket of strawberries to use as a little sewing box with a pincushion on top.
Village to hang on the Christmas tree.

SHISHA WORK
OPPOSITE:
Blue jeans and work shirt in "Shisha", or Indian mirror embroidery.

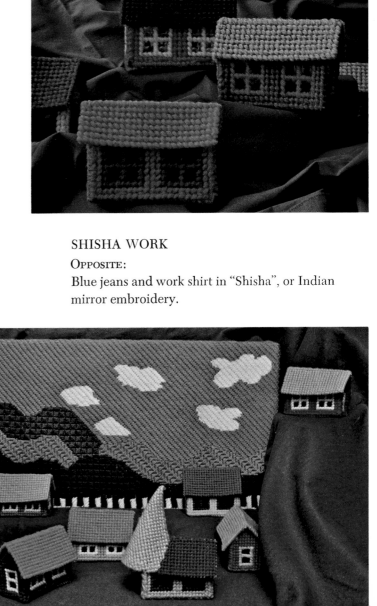

SHISHA

Shisha. It's not what you think. It has nothing to do with sneezing! Shisha is the Indian name for mirror, and in the province of Kutch in Northern India there's a tradition for a most unusual form of embroidery. Small rounds of mica or mirrors are sewn all over the embroidery, really setting them into the cloth like jewels with the stitching. As you can imagine, this produces a very rich, glittering effect as the fabric is moved about, and I think it has all sorts of exciting possibilities.

I have made bluejeans and a work shirt, which you can see on the preceding page, but this is a mere beginning. You could make a shisha evening collar, belt, or handbag, add touches of mirror embroidery to an evening skirt, or combine it with other embroidery.

The mirrors are available (see page 33) but you can also buy mylar, a linen-backed aluminum fabric, from most art stores. Then you can cut out the shapes (circles are best) and work them into your embroidery, following the instructions on page 33. The patterns for the owl family in the tree, and the birds and flowers on the bluejeans are on pages 180 and 182.

ORIENTAL GOLD

Gold thread is one of the most ancient and beautiful of embroidery materials. It's been used since biblical times, when it was beaten into flat plate and woven in with the stitches. But at some time in the distant past the Chinese discovered a wonderful way of using it. Instead of sewing down the fragile, plain gold, they wrapped it around a core of silk, making a pliable, firm thread, which was much easier to work with.

This pure gold thread will never tarnish—it is stitched down on the surface of the cloth with invisible silken stitches. This is the way those magnificent Chinese robes were done. To Western eyes the stitches are too perfect to be attained by human hands, and yet, like many other things, once you learn to make them in easy stages you find them nicely within your grasp. The effect of a flat, smooth golden fabric is obtained by stitching double rows of metal thread side by side. As you can see on the next page, imperial gleaming dragons are stitched with their golden scales like rays of light piercing the midnight blue of the silk background. The essence of Oriental art was to stay within the limitations of the materials, yet to make the most of them, and the Chinese became masters of stylization.

My jewel box is worked with the fluid lines of waves and water and is entirely couched in silver gilt threads with a scattering of sequins where the waves are cresting. Red suede cloth gives the soft effect of velvet, but is much easier to work with, since it does not fray and is easy to attach

to your wooden box later. You will find the instructions for the box on page 184.

Once you have worked with metal threads you will really have graduated to being an embroiderer par excellence. You could make an evening belt, a necklace or choker, an evening dress, a vest, a jeweled evening bag, a coat of arms, a sculptured wall hanging—the prospects are exciting and sophisticated.

Oriental gold has been placed last in this book, because it *is* easier to learn to handle more pliable and well-behaved wool yarns first. But the satisfaction of becoming a really topnotch embroiderer who has graduated to gold thread is well worth a little extra effort!

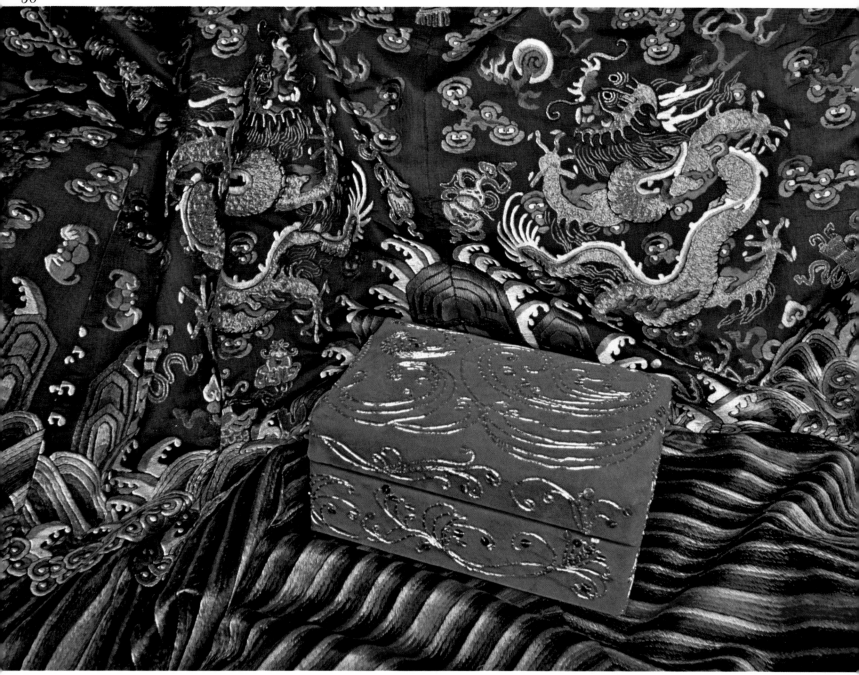

ORIENTAL GOLD
A jewel box, couched with real gold thread in the Chinese manner on red suede cloth.

LIBRARY OF NEEDLEPOINT STITCHES

On the following pages you will find a library of needlepoint stitches. There is one basic difference between needlepoint and crewel or silk embroidery. In crewel you work freely over the surface (a surface decoration). In needlepoint you work over the threads of the mesh or canvas (a surface *covering*). Therefore, your needlepoint stitches are bound by the weave of the fabric and can go only vertically, horizontally, or diagonally.

From this limited base there are literally hundreds of variations, so working with your "library" as a beginning, you can ring the changes, finding inspired combinations that can form your own geometric patterns. If you like, you can collect them all on a sampler (as on page 40). This will be useful later when you are using the stitches as backgrounds for tent-stitched needlepoint designs, or when you are using them to make a complete design on their own.

Tent Stitch and Half Cross Stitch are the most basic for needlepoint because they have the effect of woven tapestry, and fine shading can be done easily with small slanting stitches, which cover the canvas smoothly. Cross Stitch, with a square effect, slightly more textured, but similar to Tent, takes twice as long to do, but is very effective.

Apart from basic slanting stitches there are straight stitches—Gobelin, which is like Satin Stitch worked in horizontal rows on the canvas, and Brick Stitch, used in Bargello patterns (see page 124), which is simply staggered vertical stitches worked in brick fashion (hence the name).

Unbelievable as it seems, the hundreds of others are all variations of these simple upright or diagonal stitches. You can experiment with them to your heart's content, to achieve the most attractive and pleasing effects.

STARTING AND ENDING OFF

Having knotted your thread, take the needle down through the canvas, 6 or 7 threads away from where you intend to begin stitching, leaving the knot on top. Start stitching, working toward the knot, covering the long thread which lies on the reverse side. When you have worked up to the knot, cut it off—the end of the thread will be held securely under the canvas by your stitches.

When you are finished with a thread, bring it to the top of the canvas some distance from your last stitch. Leave the thread there until, as with the knot, the long thread on the back has been covered by more stitching. Cut off the end of the thread.

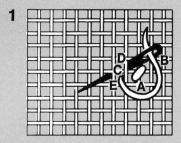

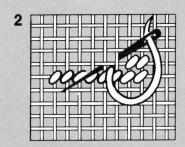

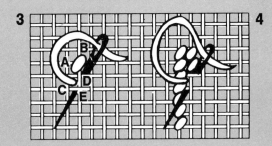

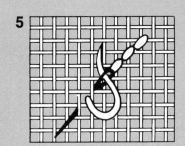

TENT STITCH/Worked horizontally
(Continental Stitch)

Starting at lower right of area to be filled, come up at A. Go down at B (*one* thread above and *one* thread to the right of A). Come up at C, one thread to the left, and level with A. Repeat, going in at D, up at E, making a horizontal row of slanting stitches, working from right to left across the canvas.

At the end of the line, turn canvas and work a second row of identical stitches above the first. Bring needle up in the same holes as the previous line of stitches, so that no canvas shows between. By turning the canvas completely around at the end of each line, the rows may *always* be worked from right to left, making it easier to the right handed to "sew" each stitch with the needle slanted as in diagrams 1 and 2. Left handed people should simply turn these diagrams upside down to follow them, beginning each area to be filled at the top left hand corner.

For effect on reverse side, see opposite.

TENT STITCH/Worked vertically
(Continental Stitch)

Tent Stitch may also be worked in vertical rows, turning the canvas so that you always work from top to bottom. Begin at the top left of the area to be filled. When worked in straight lines, Tent Stitch is often called the Continental Stitch.

For effect on reverse side, see opposite.

Sometimes it is necessary to work diagonal lines of tent stitch slanting from left to right as in the diagram. In this case the stitch becomes like a back stitch. The needle comes up one thread to the left and one thread below the last stitch, and goes down into the exact same hole as this previous stitch, as shown. To work a whole background of lines in this direction would not be smooth, as the stitches do not interlock as they do in diagrams 6, 7 and 8.

TENT STITCH/Worked diagonally (Basket Weave)

Tent Stitch may also be worked in diagonal lines. When working from top to bottom, the needle is placed vertically so that the next stitch may be taken on the true diagonal of the mesh.

When working backgrounds or large areas of one color in tent stitch, the best way to fill the shape is by working diagonally as shown here. When working from top to bottom the needle is vertical.

When working from bottom to top the needle is horizontal. This gives a basket weave effect on the back which is firm and hardwearing. The stitch is clear cut because the needle always goes *down* into the *previous* stitches, never *up* (as diagrams 2 and 4). The canvas does not have to be reversed at the end of each row (as do 1 and 3). These three reasons make it very practical for backgrounds. To learn the stitch, practice it as shown in diagrams 6 and 7 on an odd piece of canvas. Once it is understood that it is identical with horizontal and vertical tent stitch (1, 2, 3 and 4), only worked diagonally, it will be easy to work a corner.

Begin in the top right hand corner, and always work the rows alternately—first from top to bottom, and then from bottom to top, starting with one stitch, and increasing each row. Always leave a thread hanging in the middle of the row if you have to leave the canvas, then when you pick it up again you can tell whether you were working up or down. When two rows are worked in the same direction the Basket Weave on the back is interrupted; this makes an undesirable break which shows on the front.

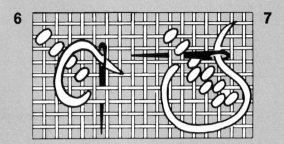

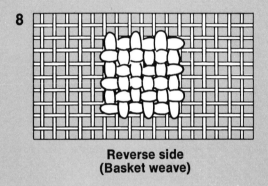

Reverse side (Basket weave)

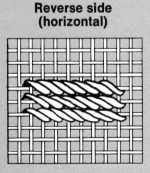

Reverse side (horizontal)

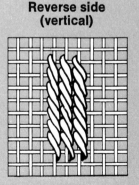

Reverse side (vertical)

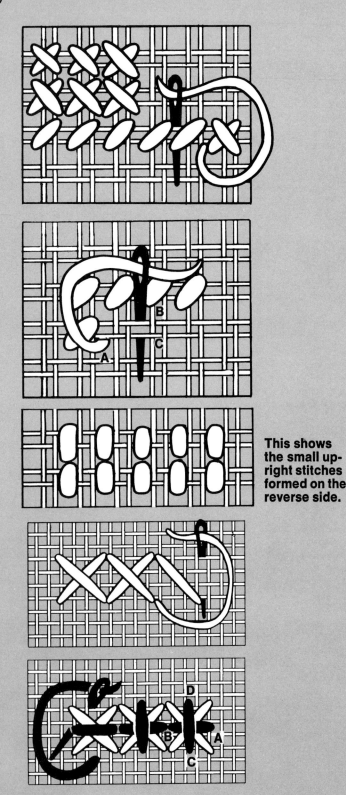

This shows the small upright stitches formed on the reverse side.

CROSS STITCH

Work a row of half cross stitches (as shown above). Then complete the cross by working back in the opposite direction, repeating the first row of stitching, and going into exactly the same holes as the previous stitches, as shown.

HALF CROSS STITCH

Come up at A, count one double thread up and one double thread over to the right, and go in at B. Come up at C, one thread immediately below B. The needle is therefore always vertical, as shown. Work to the end of the line, then turn the canvas completely upside down, and make another identical row below, fitting the new stitches into the holes made by the previous ones. Continue, turning the canvas at the end of each row.

Half cross stitch should always be worked on double thread (penelope) canvas. Because the canvas has such a firm weave, the upright stitches formed on the reverse side, cannot slip between the mesh, as they might on single or mono canvas.

DOUBLE CROSS STITCH

First make a line of cross stitch as shown.

Then, using a contrasting thread, make a series of crosses on top of the first stitches from A to B and C to D.

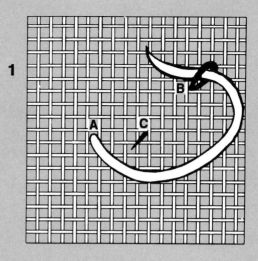

MONTENEGRIN CROSS STITCH

Come up at A, count 4 threads up and 8 threads over to the right, and go in at B. Come up at C 4 threads to the right of A and level with it.

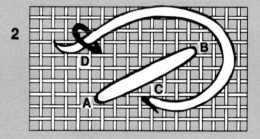

Now go in at D 4 threads directly above A and come up at C again in exactly the same hole made by the previous stitch.

Now go in at E 4 threads immediately above C and come up once again at C in the same hole.

Repeat steps 1, 2 and 3 to make a line of stitching as shown at 4.

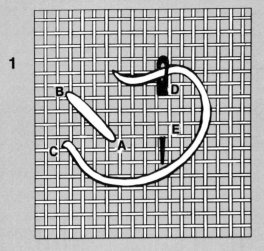

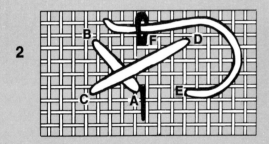

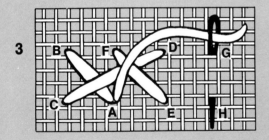

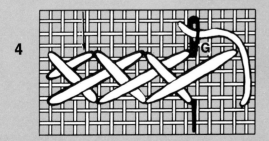

LONG-ARMED CROSS STITCH/or Twist Stitch

Working from left to right come up at A. Count 4 threads straight up and 4 threads over to the left, going down at B. Come up at C 4 threads directly below B; then go in at D 8 threads away and on a line with B. Come up at E 4 threads directly below D.

Go in at F 4 threads to the left and level with D (exactly midway between D and B). Come up in the same hole as the first stitch, at A directly below F.

Now go in at G 4 threads to the right and level with D, come up at H 4 threads directly below G.

Now repeat numbers 2 and 3 to make a continuous line of stitching as shown. Note: after the first few stitches, the needle always fits back into the same holes as the previous stitches. If necessary, an extra stitch, shown at arrow, may be slipped under the bar to complete the line.

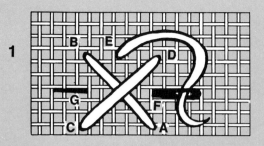

RICE STITCH

First make a cross stitch from A to B and C to D over 6 threads of the canvas. Then proceed to cross each of the four arms of the cross stitch with slanting stitches. Begin by coming up at E, midway between B and D, and go in at F, midway between D and A. Note: E and F are therefore each 3 threads away from D.

Next come up at G, halfway between B and C, and go back to E. Come up at H halfway between C and A.

Continue the pattern by going in at F and up at G.

Complete the pattern by going in at H. The needle is shown coming up at J to begin another pattern.

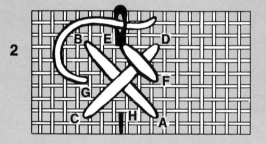

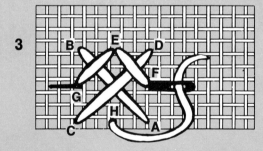

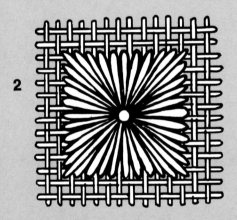

ALGERIAN EYELET

To make eyelet holes, work Satin stitches over four threads of the canvas into *one central hole* as shown in diagrams. The effectiveness of the stitch relies on the clear open hole in the center and the evenness of the stitches.

Insert scissors into hole that will be the center of the eyelet and twist so as to enlarge it, taking care not to break any of the threads.

Always go *down* in the center, rotating the needle in the hole as you take each stitch, to force it open.

Draw thread tight.

Take care to place stitches side by side, do not allow them to overlap, or the hole will close up and the stitches will not be smooth.

Shows an eyelet worked to form a diamond 1.
Shows a square eyelet 2.

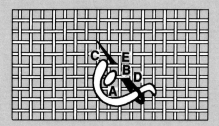

WEB STITCH

Come up at A and go down at B, making a tent stitch over one thread of the canvas. Come up at C one thread above and one thread to the left of B. Go in at D, one thread below and one thread to the right of B, making a long slanting stitch. Come up at E one thread immediately above B.

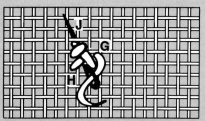

Go in at F, making a small stitch across the long slanting one, and come up at G on the other side of the stitch, one thread below and one to the right of E.

Go in at H, over the stitch, one thread to the left and one below G. Come up at J.

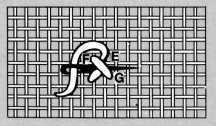

Now make another long slanting stitch, close to the previous one.

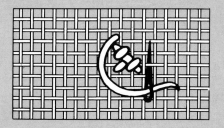

Work all the way back, placing slanting stitches across the line alternately with those of the previous row, as shown.

The finished effect has the appearance of diagonal weaving.

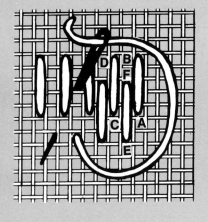
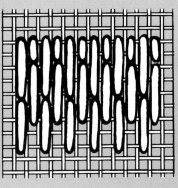

BRICK STITCH

Come up at A, go down at B, 4 threads above. Come up at C, level with A but 2 threads to the left, then down at D 4 threads directly above C. Repeat across the canvas. Work the next row beneath the first coming up at E 2 threads below and between A and C, then go down 4 threads above at F.

Finished effect showing small stitches used to fill in the top line making an even edge.

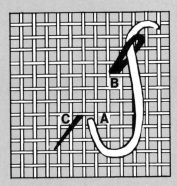
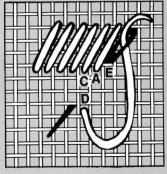

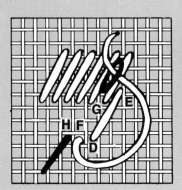
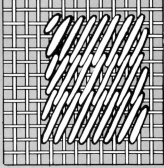

ENCROACHING GOBELIN

Come up at A. Count 4 threads straight up, and 2 threads to the right, and go in at B. Come up at C, one thread to the left and level with A, and repeat the first stitch, going in one thread to the left of B. Continue to make a horizontal row of slanting stitches.

Come up at D, 3 threads immediately below C. As before, count 4 threads straight up and 2 to the right going in at E. Note: E is one thread above and one to the right of A.

Repeat DE, making a stitch from F to G. Note: This second row of stitches encroaches into the previous row by one thread of canvas, so slide your needle carefully between the stitches at G, to locate the mesh. Come up at H, and repeat to the end of the row.

Shows the finished effect with smaller stitches at the lower right and upper left to fill out the shape as needed.

BRICK STITCH/Long and Short Variation

Come up at A, go down at B, 6 threads below. Come up at C and down at D, repeating the first stitch. Come up at E, 3 threads to the left of C. Repeat across the canvas working in pairs.

Then repeat the first row exactly, coming up 4 threads below at F, working pairs of stitches into the spaces left by the previous stitches, as in the diagram.

Fill the intervening spaces with contrasting color, covering two threads of the canvas, working into the same holes as the previous stitches.

When one color is used this stitch may be worked in horizontal lines, making two long and two short stitches alternately.

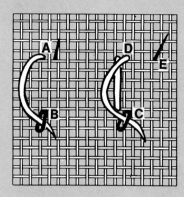

CHEVRON

Come up at A, and go down 4 threads above at B. Come up at C, one thread above and one thread to the left of A. Go in at D, 4 threads above C and one thread to the left and above B. Continue, from E to F, and G to H, going one thread higher with each stitch, always going over 4 threads, as shown.

Then work downwards (from J to K, L to M, N to O) with each new stitch one thread below the previous one as shown. Continue, making this chevron pattern across the canvas.

Repeat below, making a row of stitches identical with the previous ones, but over 2 threads, fitting into the holes of the previous row.

Finished effect of chevron bandings of long and short stitches worked alternately.

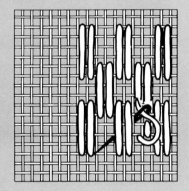

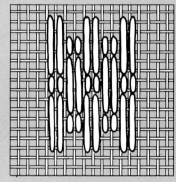

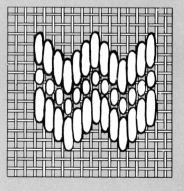

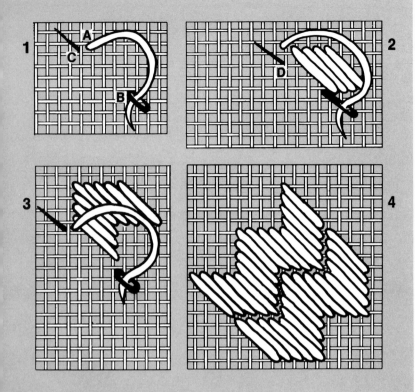

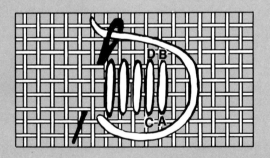

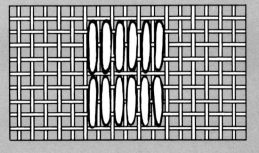

STEP STITCH

1. Come up at A, count 4 threads down and 4 threads over, and go down at B. Come up at C, one thread to the left and level with A.

2. Repeat, taking 5 stitches side by side. After taking the fifth stitch, come up at D, one thread immediately below the last stitch.

3. Repeat this stitch, making 5 stitches side by side vertically. Then repeat the first diagram again.

4. This forms a series of steps descending diagonally. If you cover the whole area with rows of this pattern, start in an open part of the area so that you can first establish the pattern before filling in small areas at the edge.

STRAIGHT GOBELIN STITCH

Come up at A, and go down at B 4 threads above. Repeat, from C to D, one thread to the left, and continue making a row of vertical stitches the same size, side by side.

Make another row of vertical stitches underneath the first, fitting the stitches back into exactly the same holes as those formed by the stitches of the previous row. When working these upright stitches, use more threads of yarn than when you work slanting ones, in order to cover the canvas. Do not pull too tightly or spaces will form between the rows, showing bare threads of canvas. If this happens, cover the spaces by working a line of back stitch (see page 12) between each row after the whole area is filled.

ORIENTAL STITCH

1. Come up at A. Count 2 threads over and 2 threads up, go in at B. Repeat, making 4 stitches vertically, one above the other. On the fifth stitch count 5 stitches up and 5 stitches over, and take a long diagonal stitch.

Take the next stitch above 4 threads up and 4 threads over.

2. Then take the next 3 threads up and 3 over.

3. Finally, work the last stitch 2 up and 2 over and continue making a horizontal row of 4 diagonal stitches.

4. Complete the pattern by working rows side by side, into the same holes as each on the previous row, as in the diagram.

BARGELLO (method of working)

The essence of Bargello is its smooth flat effect. To keep this, always work with the shortest stitch possible on the reverse side. For instance, if you pass over 4 threads on the front, pick up only 2 on the back, as in the diagram. Only when blocks of stitches are worked side by side should you carry the needle across the back coming up on one side, down on the other, like Satin Stitch.

1. Note that when the line of stitching slants upwards, the needle slants down.

2. To maintain a short stitch at the back, the process is reversed on the way down, when the needle slants upwards.

3. Reverse side shows short stitches.

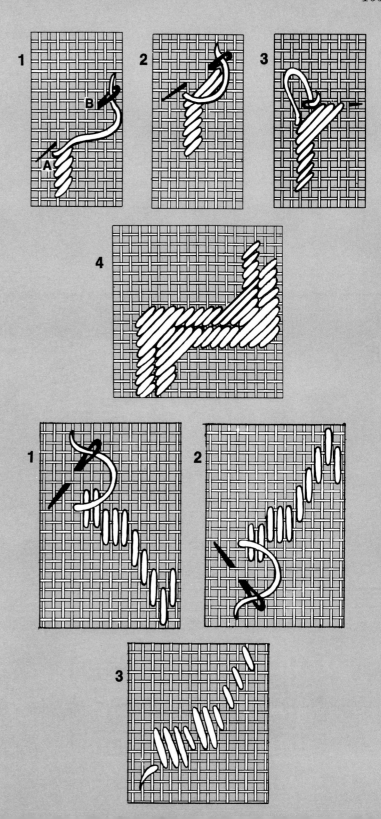

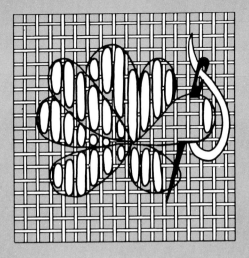

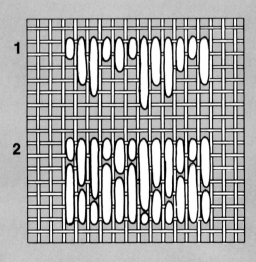

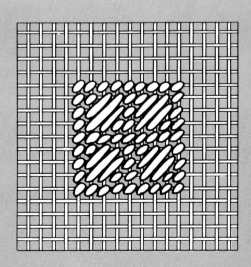

CREWEL-POINT STITCHES

STRAIGHT STITCH

As shown in the Garden of Eden design on page 65, this straight Satin Stitch may be worked across the shortest area of the shape to be filled, working either vertically or horizontally (whichever gives the shortest stitch). Come up on one outline and go down on the other side, working smooth stitches side by side. Make sure the canvas is covered and no canvas threads show between the stitches. On wide areas it may be best to divide the shape into two or more rows of stitches, as in the photo. A neater effect is obtained if you always work either vertically or horizontally, never diagonally.

RANDOM BARGELLO

The background of a tapestry worked in Straight Stitch may be left open, with the bare canvas contrasting well with the close stitching (as shown here and on page 65). Alternatively it may be filled with Random Brick stitches, as shown here and on page 64.

1. Work a row of Long and Short stitches, making each stitch an irregular length.

2. Fit the next row into the first one agan, making each stitch irregular. Never take a stitch longer than 6 threads, as it might catch when the needlepoint is in use.

SCOTTISH STITCH

Work vertical and horizontal rows of Tent Stitch (page 98), forming boxes of 5 stitches each. Fill these squares with 5 slanting Satin Stitches, as in the diagram.

SQUARED FILLING

1. Work Parisian Stitch (one vertical stitch over two threads, one over 4, one over 2, etc.) over the area.

2. With a contrasting color, lay long diagonal lines from one side to the other, first in one direction, then in the other. Lay them on the natural diagonal lines that appear in the pattern, formed by the Parisian Stitch. With another contrasting color (or the Parisian Stitch color), hold these diagonal stitches flat with a small vertical stitch over each intersection.

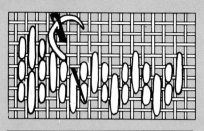

WEAVING

Lay long, vertical stitches from one side to the other of the area to be covered, with 2 threads of canvas between each. In the opposite direction weave under and over these threads, 2 lines together, as in the diagram. Except at the edges, the needle does not pass through the canvas—the weaving is all done on the surface.

CHAIN

Follow the instructions for Chain Stitch on page 14, working over the canvas in whichever direction you want, treating the canvas as though it was embroidery linen.

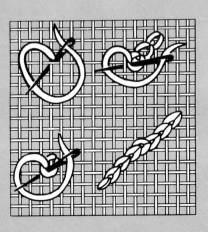

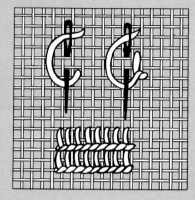

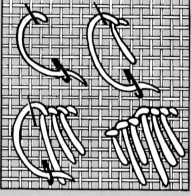

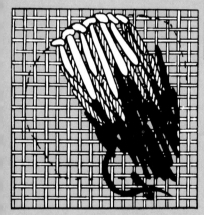

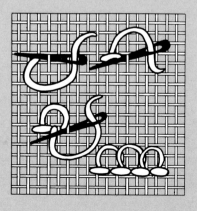

ROWS OF BUTTONHOLE STITCH

Work horizontal rows of Buttonhole Stitch, following the instructions on page 17. Start the first row at the base, and work upward, with the loops of each succeeding row overlapping the top of the previous row, as in the diagram.

BUTTONHOLE WITH LONG AND SHORT

Work a row of Buttonhole, as shown in the diagrams, quite freely over the canvas without counting the mesh. Then work Long and Short stitches into this first row, blending the colors row by row, as on page 76. Do not attempt to count threads.

TURKEY STITCH

Work in horizontal rows, taking up one thread of canvas with each stitch as in the diagram. Turkey Work on canvas is worked in exactly the same way as Turkey Work in crewel (page 31).

YOUR "EMBROIDERY COOK BOOK"

On the following pages you will find the "recipes" or instructions to follow for making the various things shown in this book. Just as you would when you follow a recipe, at first you will want to stay closely to the original, following the instructions step by step. But as you begin to feel free and easy within the medium, you can add your own ingredients, just using my suggestions as a base for your own experiments.

All the designs in this book are shown in color, so you may either follow them exactly, or make your own color scheme to suit your individual requirements.

Wherever possible, the designs are life size, and you can trace them right from the book. Each design which has to be enlarged is shown with a light gray grid. To enlarge them all you have to do is to take a *square* piece of tracing paper of approximately your desired finished size, fold it into eight squares (by creasing the paper in half, and half again, etc.) and draw your design in larger scale by fitting each section of the pattern into the larger squares exactly as it appears in the smaller ones. Needlepoint designs, to be counted out from graphs, can be enlarged or reduced, depending upon the size of canvas mesh on which they are worked.

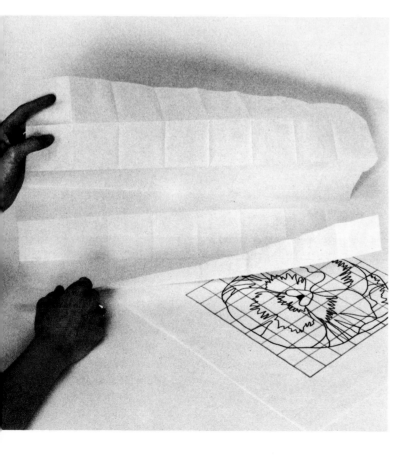

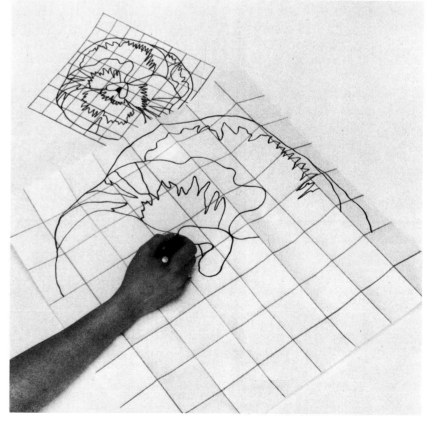

GEOMETRIC NEEDLEPOINT/Tennis Racquet Cover

Color, page 46.

MATERIALS NEEDED

Tennis racquet cover, pre-made for needlepoint
4 shades Persian wool
#18 tapestry needle

HOW TO GO ABOUT IT

The racquet cover was worked on a ready-made cover with a blank canvas in front, ready for needlepoint.

Start by lightly running a pencil between the mesh of the canvas in the middle of the cover, vertically and horizontally. Once you have established the center in this way, you can start the pattern at this point at the base of one of the "V's" of the design. Then the design will be balanced with equal pattern on either side, and at the top and bottom. Use 2 threads of yarn on #12 canvas, and work Gobelin Stitch (page 108) over 4 threads of the canvas. Note carefully where the stitch decreases, to form the "ribbon" effect.

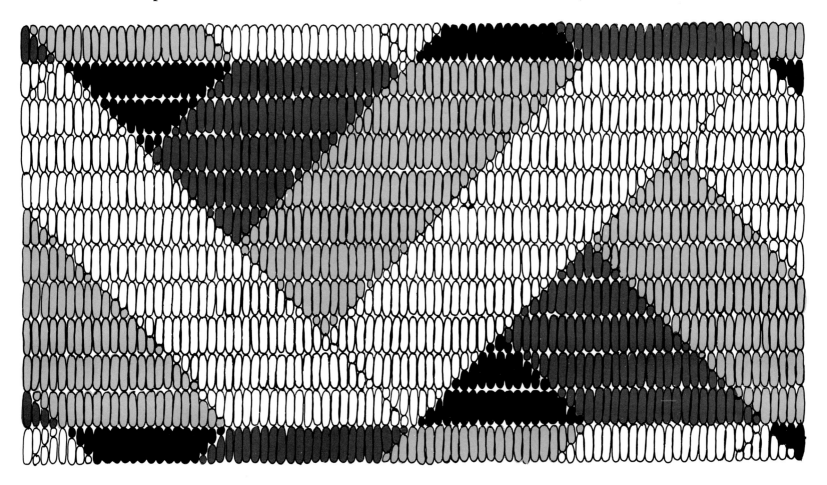

GEOMETRIC NEEDLEPOINT/Bolster

Color, page 46; mounting, page 187.

MATERIALS NEEDED

½ yd. of canvas #10 or #12
4 shades of one color and 4 shades of a contrasting
    color
#18 tapestry needle
½ yd. velvet for edging and finishing
2 large flat buttons covered with matching velvet
1 yd. piping cord
Dacron stuffing

See diagram below.

HOW TO GO ABOUT IT

    With a pencil, mark a square 14″ x 14″ in the
center of your canvas. Using three threads of Persian on either #10 or #12 canvas work ascending
straight stitches over 4 threads of the mesh (each
successive stitch overlaps the previous one by 2
threads). Start with either the darkest or lightest
of one of the groups of 4 colors, and work the
whole band, shading from dark to light or vice
versa. Then, following the diagram, work the band
that descends in the opposite direction, using the
other group of 4 colors. When the whole area has
been covered, fill in the 4 stitches that form a
diamond between each band, using a dark color.

See diagram opposite.

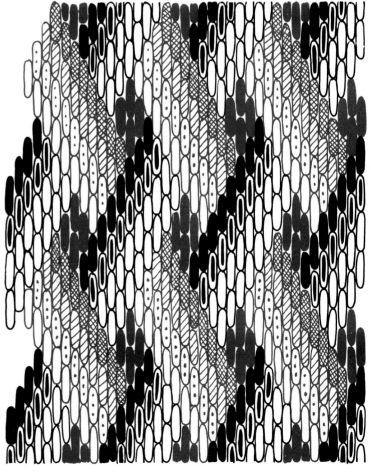

GEOMETRIC NEEDLEPOINT/Handbags

Color, page 46.

MATERIALS NEEDED

Ready-made handbag or shoulder bag, with plain
  canvas flap for needlepoint
Persian wool
#18 tapestry needle

HOW TO GO ABOUT IT

It is important to keep these handbags flat and
tailored looking, so it is helpful to baste them to
the top of a ring frame for working, since they
cannot easily be fitted *into* one. Then you can
work with even tension and the bag flap may only
need pressing afterwards. (It is hard to block the
finished needlepoint, though if it should be necessary, this is best done face down on a board with
a power stapler, holding the needlework firmly
around the edges. The staples can be put in lightly
so they will not leave any marks and will be easy
to remove.) Both bags are worked in Gobelin
Stitch (page 108) with very different effects. On
the handbag you can make your own arrangement
of initials, using the ideas on pages 118 and 119,
and working over three threads of the mesh. The
end result can be every bit as chic as a Gucci or
Louis Vuitton bag, but your *own* personal mono-
gram is used instead of theirs. The design on the
shoulder bag can be used equally well on anything
else—it's a bold, simple design that can look dra-
matically different, depending on your color
scheme. Just count it out from the graph on the
opposite page, using 6 colors and working over 6,
12, or 2 threads of the canvas, according to the
pattern.

On both bags experiment with a few actual-size
stitches before you begin to decide how many
threads of wool to use. The stitches should not
look bulky, but neither should the canvas show
between them. Once a few stitches have been
worked it will be easy to tell.

Initialed handbag. See alphabet, pages 118-119.

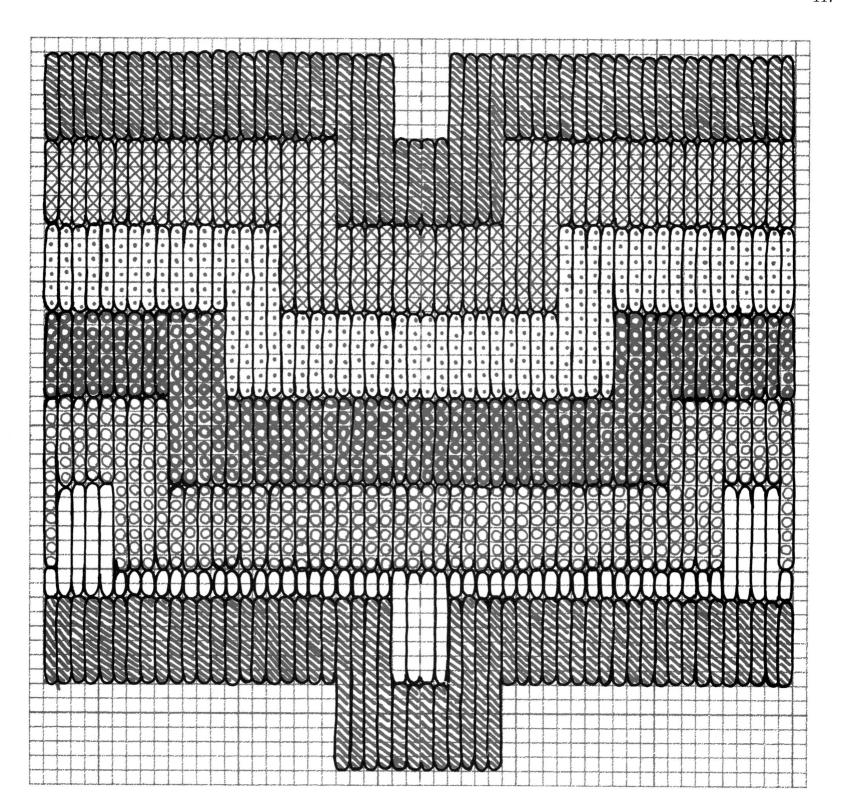

118

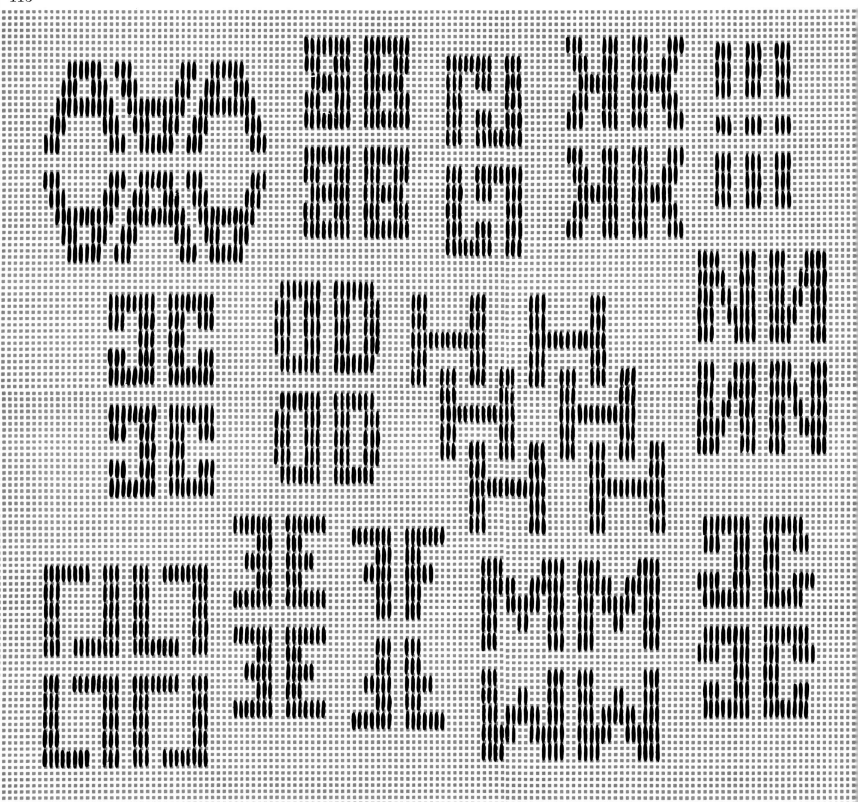

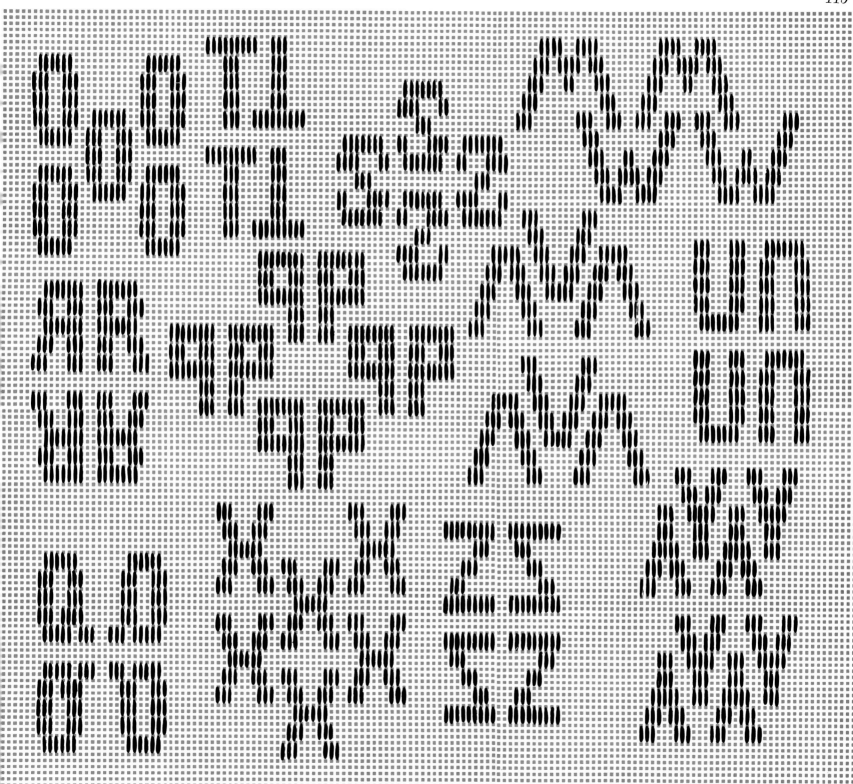

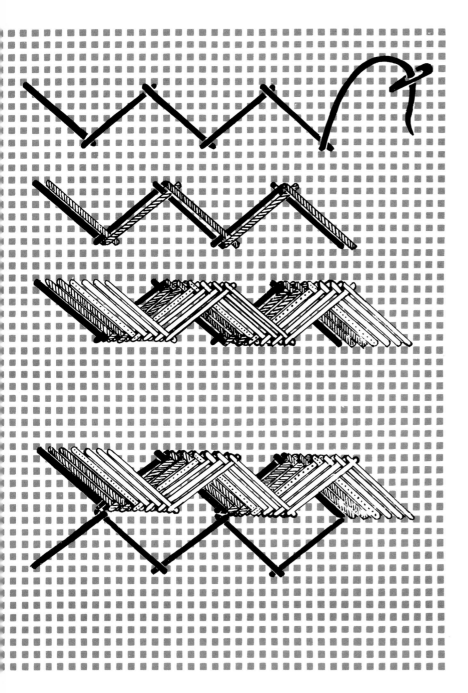

HONEYCOMB STITCH

Color, page 46.

MATERIALS NEEDED

Linen drawstring bag
2 sheets plastic canvas
Acrylic or Persian yarn
DMC cotton embroidery floss
#18 tapestry needle

HOW TO GO ABOUT IT

A "collar" of Honeycomb-stitched plastic canvas was applied to the drawstring bag, but Honeycomb Stitch may be used for any other suitable canvas design.

NOTE: Although it is worked horizontally, the finished design is best turned vertically to give a honeycomb effect. (See photo.)

1. Using 2 threads of dark Persian yarn on plastic or #10 canvas, work a row of Herringbone Stitch. Count 5 threads down and 6 over to make the first diagonal. Come up 1 thread to the left, level with the last stitch, and repeat, slanting at the opposite angle. Continue along the line.

2. Repeat the first row, working with a shade lighter beside it, one thread away.

3. Continue, repeating so that the final band has 1 row of dark, 2 of medium, 1 of medium light, and 2 of the lightest color. Repeat in the opposite direction below, working directly under the first dark row, coming up in the same holes as this row, as in the diagram. Continue, to complete

this row, giving the effect shown in the diagram. Now with contrasting wool or cotton floss, fill in the open space left between the stitches with vertical Satin Stitch. To make the stitches fill the area well, it is sometimes necessary to pull back the stitching gently with your needle, as shown in the diagram.

Finished effect, turned vertically.

start

KALEIDOSCOPE PILLOW

Color, page 58.

MATERIALS NEEDED

½ yd. #10 canvas, 36″ wide (finished size approx. 14″ x 14″)

6 shades of Persian wool, approx. 6 oz. total (use 4 threads)

#18 tapestry needle

HOW TO GO ABOUT IT

Cut a square of canvas 18″ x 18″. This will give you 2 inches extra all around your pillow for turnbacks.

It is important to know that canvas mesh is never square, therefore if you *measure* a square, mark it on the canvas, and then try to count your pattern out to fit inside it—only frustration will result! A finished counted design will always come out very slightly wider than it is high, or higher than it is wide, depending on which way you are looking at it. So start by establishing the center guide lines (see at left). Count the pattern out following the graph opposite, and you will have no trouble!

To establish the center, fold your 18″ x 18″ piece of canvas in half and in half again, and crease the folds. Run a pencil between the threads of the canvas, along the crease lines, vertically and horizontally. (NOTE: Borders and guide lines on canvas are always best marked lightly with a pencil, never with permanent ink. The latter becomes too heavy, is messy if you make a mistake, and might show through your wool if you decided later to work beyond the edges of the pattern you have marked. Pencil, if marked lightly enough, will never show, can be erased if necessary, and the pencil easily stays within the grooves of the canvas for drawing straight lines.)

Once you have the straight lines on the canvas you must draw the diagonals. Place the canvas on a table. Kneel so that you are at eye level with it. By maneuvering the canvas slightly, raised diagonal lines where the mesh interweaves will become clear. Lay a ruler beside the diagonal that bisects the center and rule this 45-degree line with a pencil. Repeat on the opposite side.

Now that you have the canvas marked as in the diagram, you are ready to mark off each of the *straight* lines in blocks of 4 as shown. Start in the center, and first count 2 threads, then blocks of 4, marking each with a pencil until you have 20 blocks of 4. Using the darkest shade of your range of colors, come up on the 46th thread out from the center (that is, 1 block of 2, 11 blocks of 4) and go down 4 threads away (toward the edge). Come up 2 threads below the top of the first stitch and to the left of it, and continue, following the method of Bargello stitching described on page 109. When you have worked out to the corner, following the diagram opposite, go down on the diagonal line. Repeat from the center line, working out to the right-hand diagonal. Then repeat this exactly on the other three sides until you have a line going around the square as in the diagram. Then work round and round, following the pattern first inside this line, then outside it, alternating lighter and darker shades as in the photograph.

For blocking and mounting the pillow, turn to page 186.

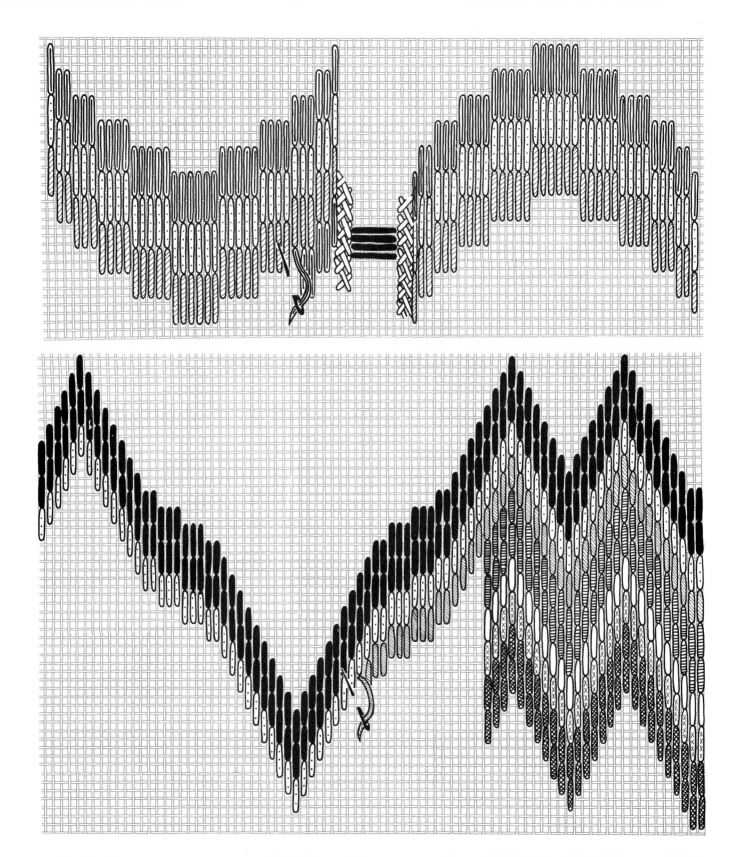

BARGELLO PATTERNS

Color, pages 58, 59.

MATERIALS NEEDED

#12 canvas (used on all these Bargello patterns)
Persian wool
#18 tapestry needle
Twisted crochet cotton (for pattern at the top of
    page 124)

HOW TO GO ABOUT IT

All these Bargello patterns were worked in the way shown on page 109. The essence of Bargello is its flat, smooth effect. To maintain this, always work with the shortest stitch possible on the reverse side. For instance, if you pass over 4 threads on the front, pick up only 2 threads on the back, as in the diagrams on page 109. This may seem confusing to those taught to use as much thread as possible, for better wear, when working Tent Stitch (Continental or Basket Weave, page 98). But the stitches on the reverse side of Bargello would become so long they would wear less well, and the long, exposed threads, double the length of those on the front, would also tend to make the needle-work thick and bulky. Only when the blocks of stitches are worked side by side should you carry the needle across the back, coming up on one side and going on the other, as in the Satin Stitch of crewel embroidery.

Establish the center of each design, just as you did in the Kaleidoscope pillow on the preceding page, and start all the patterns in the middle so that they will be equally balanced on either side. My Bargello sofa pattern at the top of the page was inspired by watered silk. Twist Stitch (page 102) is worked between the bands and Satin Stitch between the Twist Stitch (page 18).

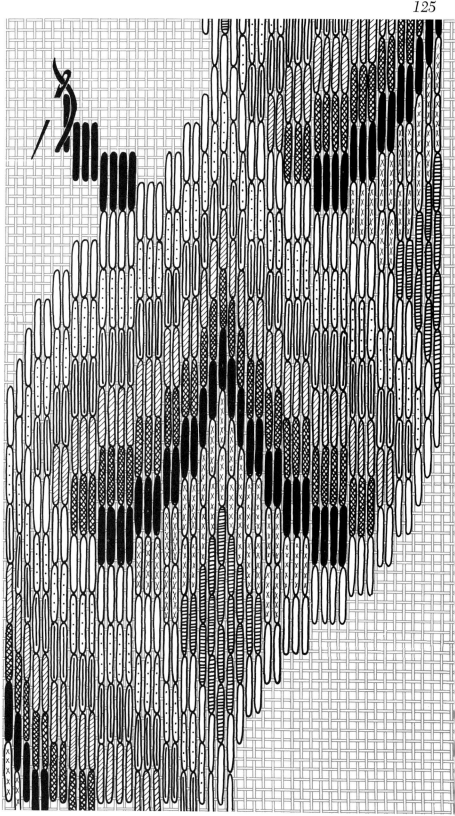

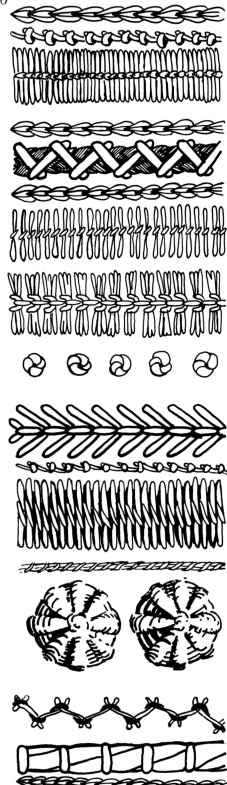

Top of mirror frame.

MIRROR FRAME

Color, page 35

Frame 18″ x 20″   Mirror 10″ x 12″

MATERIALS NEEDED

Heavy wool—corduroy or printed striped fabric
#18 chenille needle
Persian wool
Round embroidery frame

HOW TO GO ABOUT IT

1. Cut out a template or pattern in graph paper the correct size of your finished mirror frame.

2. Lay this straight on the fabric, with selvedge running parallel vertically. Catch it down here and there with masking tape to hold it in place, and rule lines all around lightly with a fine-tipped permanent marker (pencil is preferable if it will show up on your fabric). Save the pattern for mounting later.

3. Cut fabric, leaving 4″ all around for turnbacks. Oversew the edges to prevent fraying while working.

4. Using 3 and sometimes 6 strands of Persian wool (depending on your background fabric), work all the stitches across the upper edge of the frame, leaving open spaces of fabric for contrast (see diagram on this page and stitch library on pages 12–33). Work a few stitches in each row so that you can see the effect of the whole thing before it is completed. Since your stitches and textures will be varied, it may be easier to limit your colors to shades of only one or two colors for the maximum effect.

STITCHES ON WOOL FABRIC FROM TOP TO BOTTOM

Chain, Coral, Satin Stitch held flat with Split Stitch, Chain, Satin held flat with Herringbone, Chain, Roumanian Stitch (worked openly), Raised Chain, French Knots, Open Fishbone, Coral, Roumanian (worked closely), Couching, Whipped Spiders' Webs, Interlaced Herringbone, Couching, Split Stitch.

THE BOXES

Color, page 34.

MATERIALS NEEDED

2 10½″ x 13½″ sheets plastic canvas for
   box measuring 5″ x 5″ x 5½″
Acrylic yarn
Felt for lining
#18 tapestry needle

HOW TO GO ABOUT IT

First cut six pieces of plastic canvas; 2 pieces 5″ x 5″ for base; top and
4 5½″ H x 5″ W for the sides of the box. (Then you can lash the stiff
plastic to any embroidery frame and work with both hands for speed).
Work the 4 sides with vertical stripes of stitches, as listed here and shown
on page 34. Work the top and bottom with bands of Tent Stitch shaded
from dark to light in the center, as on page 34. Line each piece with felt
cut a *fraction* smaller than the finished size, hemming it to the reverse side
by catching it invisibly into the stitching here and there. Sew all the pieces
together with the Long-Armed Cross or Twist Stitch shown on page 102.
Holding the 2 pieces together, sew through them both with Twist Stitch,
1 thread in from the edge. On the top of the box, cover the 3 open sides
with the same stitch worked as an edging.

Finally, make a tassel by wrapping thread around your four fingers,
binding it tightly two-thirds of the way up, trimming it evenly and attaching a thread firmly to the top of it, as in the diagram. Sew this in place
as a handle for opening the box.

STITCHES ON PLASTIC CANVAS FROM TOP TO BOTTOM

Slanting Satin Stitch, Coral, Slanting Satin squares, Slanting Satin,
Weaving, Satin held flat with Stem Stitch, Coral, Fishbone, Roumanian,
Satin Stitches with Fishbone, Long Satin held flat with Chain, French Knots,
Fishbone, Close Herringbone.

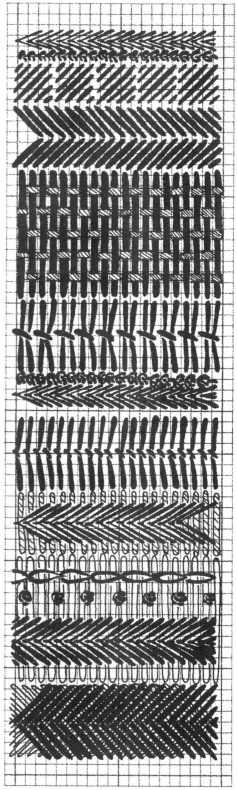

Top of box sides.

PANSY PILLOWS

Color, page 39.

MATERIALS NEEDED

½ yd. #12 canvas (finished size approx. 14″ x 14″)
Persian wool (use 4 threads)
#18 tapestry needle

HOW TO GO ABOUT IT

Have the designs opposite and on pages 130–131 enlarged photostatically, or enlarge them by the squaring method shown on page 113. Or use an opaque projector, a machine that will project your image on a screen or wall any size you desire, so that you can trace the outlines. Of the three methods, photostating is the easiest, and if the design is not to be enlarged or reduced tremendously, it is reasonably priced. It is only necessary to give the photostat studio *one* measurement—decide on the size you want the finished width or height to be and the rest of the design will follow in proportion.

The pansies are in Encroaching Gobelin (page 108). They could also be worked in Tent Stitch, but the long, vertical Gobelin stitches blend the colors together very well, which gives the velvety effect of pansy petals. Keep all the stitches vertical, and notice that stitches of adjoining petals share the same holes. This makes a clear dividing line between each petal which can easily be neatened by working a smooth, flowing row of Stem Stitch on top (see page 13). Work the Turkey Work last, keeping the rows of stitching close together to give a thick tufted effect.

Mount the pillow with a "boxing" or band of fabric 2 inches wide all around between the face of the pillow and the back. Velvet is an excellent backing fabric, and piping is not necessary, as it detracts from the "flower-head" effect.

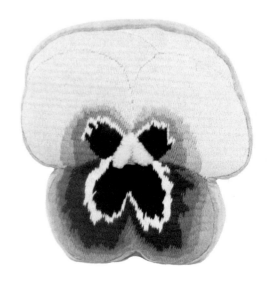

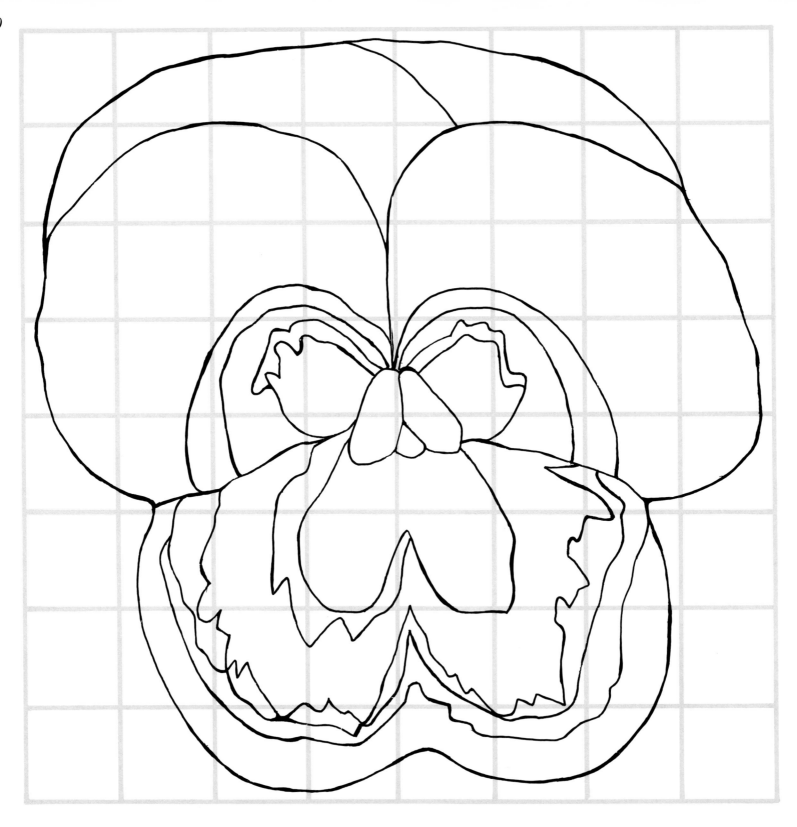

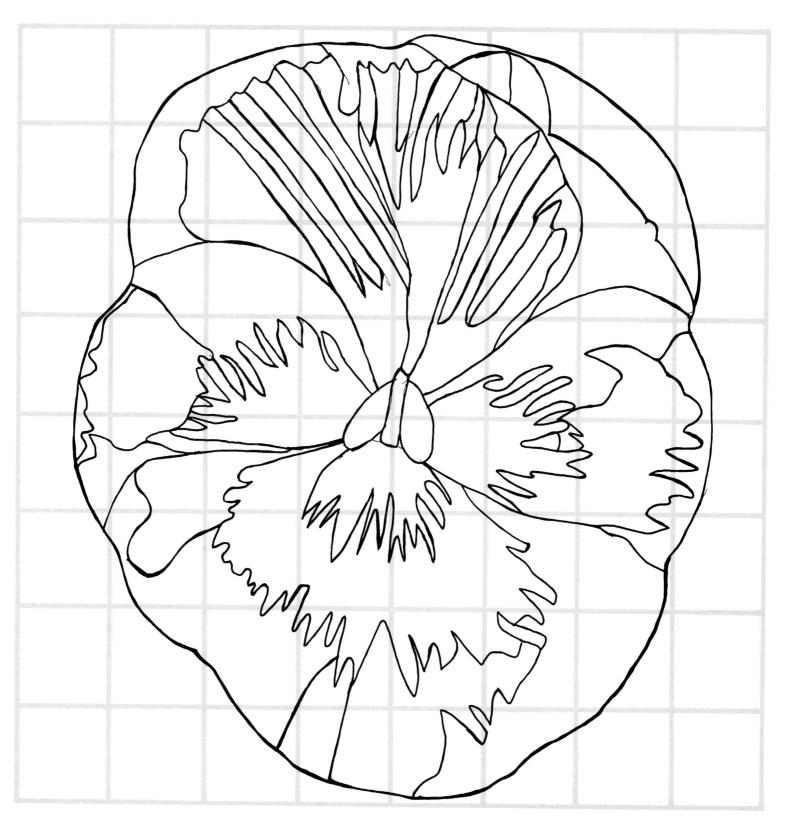

CHRISTMAS TREE

Color, page 42.

MATERIALS NEEDED

Foam "cone" size approximately 13″ x 4″
Persian wool, dark and bright greens, and bright
    "jewel" colors (use 2 and 3 threads)
½ yd. white fine-weave linen
#18 tapestry needle
#18 chenille needle

HOW TO GO ABOUT IT

Enlarge the pattern to fit your cone, as described on page 129. Trace the design in black ink on tracing paper. Then apply the design as described below.

APPLYING THE DESIGN WITH CARBON PAPER

Use only dressmaker's carbon (ordinary carbon will smudge). Fold the material in half and then in half again, and crease the folds so that they show clearly. Then smooth the material flat on a table or board and hold it down evenly with masking tape on all four sides. A really smooth, hard surface is necessary.

Fold the design into four equal parts, open it up, and lay it down on top, aligning the fold lines of the design and fabric. Now slide a sheet of carbon paper face downward between paper and material. Use blue carbon for light materials, white for dark ones. Anchor the paper with some heavy weights (books, paperweights, etc.) and trace round the outline very heavily with a pencil. Using weights is a better idea than taping the design all around, because you can lift a corner occasionally to see how well the carbon is transferring. You really must *press down* heavily to get good results, but you will soon find this out as you work.

ORDER OF WORKING

1. Stretch the design in an embroidery frame and begin by working the leaves in Satin and Straight Stitches. Using 3 threads, work with the darker greens first, overlapping the outlines of the leaves to make the effect of pine needles. Highlight some of the leaves afterward with a few straight stitches in yellow-green and light, bright blue-green. Keep all the stitches long and slanting for a thick, raised effect, working close to or over the outlines of the flowers with the leaf stitches.

2. Using 2 threads, work all the flower petals and small royal-blue circles in Padded Satin Stitch, following the direction lines in the diagram. The centers are in French Knots.

3. Using 2 threads, work larger circles in whipped and woven Spiders' Webs in bright colors on top of the previous stitching where necessary, to give a rich, padded effect.

4. Work "star" flowers in Bullion Knots, using 2 threads. When complete, block the embroidery, cut it out, leaving 1″ all around. With right sides together, match bands and sew side seam close to the needlework. Then turn it right side out and slip it over the cone. Neaten the base by hemming a circle of linen around, push a dowel through the center for the "trunk," and if you wish, "plant" it in a small flower pot with sand to keep it firm.

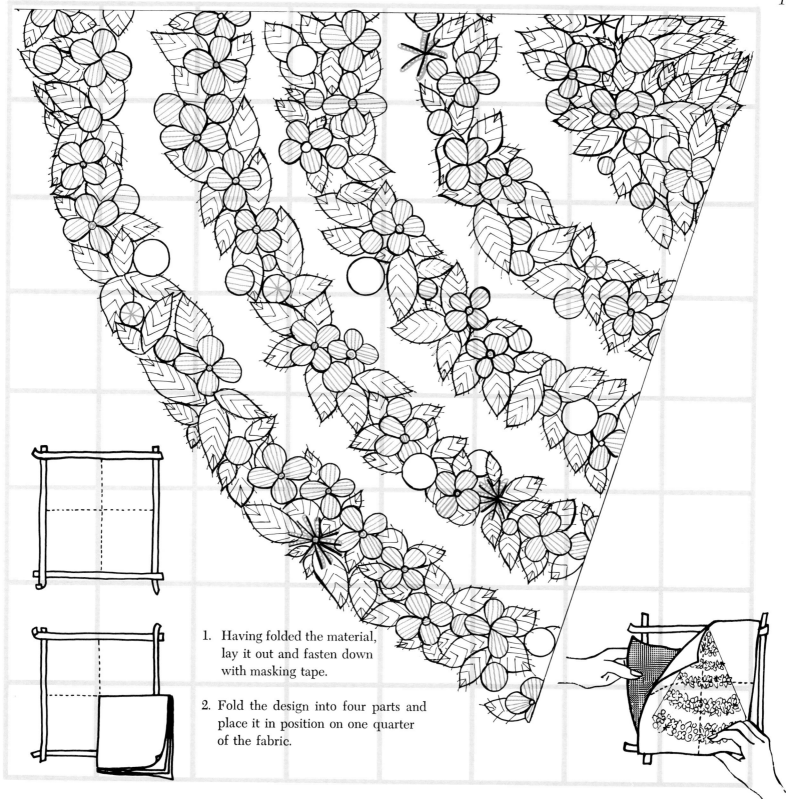

1. Having folded the material, lay it out and fasten down with masking tape.

2. Fold the design into four parts and place it in position on one quarter of the fabric.

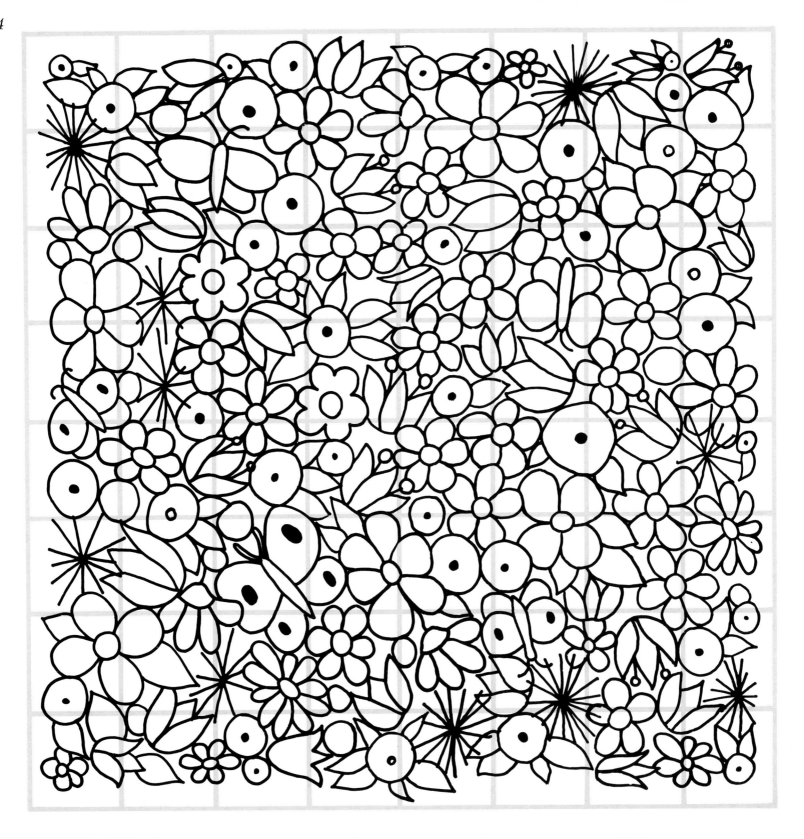

GRAPHICS FROM A TO Z

Color, page 43.

MATERIALS NEEDED

Cardboard and tracing paper

Cotton embroidery floss in brilliant colors (use 4 threads)

#20 chenille needle or #4 crewel

Fine, felt-tipped permanent marker

Bed sheet, pillowslip, or article to be monogrammed

Finished size: Letters 10″, Pillow 12″ x 14″

HOW TO GO ABOUT IT

Books of typefaces, magazines, and newspapers are all excellent sources for unusual letters. Once you have found the ones you want to use, have them photostatically enlarged to the size you need. My particular "flower letters" on the sheet turnback (shown on pages 43 and 44) measured 10 inches high. (You need them to be tall for dramatic impact and bold color—they really make everyone sit up and take notice!)

If you are ambitious enough to draw your own letters, use graph paper—it's so easy to keep your lines straight and even. Next, outline your letters on thin cardboard (laundry-shirt cardboard is good—it's easy to cut). Cut them out and lay your letters on the sheet or fabric, which has been taped down to a firm, hard surface, and trace around them, using a hard "H" pencil or a *fine*-tipped permanent felt marker. With the same marker you can work as follows:

1. Fill the whole letter with flowers and butterflies drawn free-hand, following life size drawings opposite, and the letter on page 44; or

2. Follow the method on page 155, tracing the flowers on paper, basting the tracing down to your stretched fabric, embroidering through both layers and tearing the paper away afterwards; or

3. Transfer the flowers inside the silhouette of the letter, using the carbon paper method on page 133.

The heart pillow is a good companion for the sheet, and could be personalized on the back, again as described on page 155. The pillow was worked on blue sailcloth or denim with one thread of Persian wool, but it would be equally attractive done in cotton floss to match the sheet. The stitches for both sheet and pillow are Padded Satin, French Knots, Bullion Knots, and Fishbone Stitch. Make up the pillow, using eyelet ruffle as in the photo following the instructions on page 186.

DESIGNING NEEDLEPOINT

Color, page 51.

MATERIALS NEEDED

¾ yd. #7 interlocked canvas
Persian "shag" rug wool (slightly finer than regular Persian rug wool)
   approx. 8 oz.
#13 rug needle

HOW TO GO ABOUT IT

First enlarge the design opposite (photostatically) to the size you require and transfer it according to the instructions on page 49. Alternatively, count it out from the chart on the opposite page. When you are working from a chart the easiest way is to work across in horizontal lines, as you might when hooking a rug, putting in the required number of stitches in each color as you work each line. You can work on a square frame, keeping several needles threaded, each with a different color, to leave hanging in their position on the top of the frame, and to use as you need them. Another method is to count out one "wave" at a time, starting with the darkest color and finishing one section completely before going to the next.

You can work the design in Tent Stitch (page 98) for extra hard wear, or if you want to save wool you can use half Cross Stitch when you work on Penelope (double thread) or interlocked canvas (page 6). Begin and end off as described on page 97, block your finished work as described on page 186, and mount the pillow as described on page 187.

Colors: from top to bottom, on opposite page:

White	Bright orange-red	Peach
Black	Magenta	Sand
Dark brown	Gold	Champagne
Khaki	Medium orange-red	

BORDERS, BANDINGS, AND BELL PULLS

See page 52.

MATERIALS NEEDED

Wool—Persian, English crewel, French Broder Medici (available in small skeins of assorted colors). Any of these may be used, singly or mixed together. Colors to suit your needs.

Linen twill, fine-weave linen, or closely woven fabric suitable for curtains

#18 chenille, or #3 or #4 crewel needle

HOW TO GO ABOUT IT

The great advantage of designs in narrow bandings is that they can be used alone, as luggage-rack straps, curtain tiebacks, or bell pulls, or can be embroidered and appliquéd to another fabric such as drapery borders, bedspread edgings, or "boxings" (the bandings which go around pillows, stools, benches, etc.).

To transfer the design, use the carbon-paper method shown on page 133. The thickness of wool can vary according to your stitches—for instance, two threads for French Knots, Bullion Knots, Fishbone Stitch etc.; one thread for Satin Stitch, fine Stems and Outlines, the criss-cross lines of squared fillings, etc. The stitches, starting at the top left, are as follows:

Pomegranate: Fishbone, Satin, Stem, Squared Filling

Mouse: Split, Buttonhole, Bullion Knots, Stem

Pointed petals: Fishbone, Padded Satin, Chain

Porcupine: Bullion Knots, Split, Stem, French Knots

Carnation: Chain, Block Shading, Stem

Bird in Nest: Laidwork with Seeding, Chain, Stem, Padded Satin

Leaves: Satin, Long and Short, Open Fishbone, Close Fishbone, Seeding

Pressing is often the most practical way of finishing such a long strip. Press on the wrong side with several layers of soft toweling underneath and a damp pressing cloth on top, airing frequently to allow the steam to escape.

DESIGNS FROM CHINA/Table Mat

Color, page 55.

MATERIALS NEEDED

Even-weave white linen
Each mat finished size, 13″ x 18″; cut size, 17″ x
   22″
Blue cotton embroidery floss (12 threads for the
   Cross Stitch and mat edging, 6 threads for out-
   lines and other stitching)
#18 tapestry needle
Stretcher frame, 16″ x 22″

HOW TO GO ABOUT IT

First, trace the full-size pattern on this page on to tracing paper with a fairly broad black marker (the lines should be bold). Cut your linen to the size above, and with a hard (H) pencil rule a line 3″ in from the edge all around (or if you prefer, mark the corners only, and baste a line all around exactly on the thread). Transfer the design by back-lighting—an excellent technique for transferring designs accurately (which is fully described on the next page).

NOTE: if your linen is bold and evenly woven, you need not transfer the "crosses," just trace the outlines of the blossoms, and count out the crosses on the fabric later as you stitch.

ORDER OF WORKING

First, work the Cross stitches (page 170) making sure all the slanting stitches on top are angled in the same direction. Next, work the flower outlines in Stem Stitch (page 13) and the centers in Spiders' Webs (page 32). Finally, turn the hems to the *right* side—(they should be 1 inch deep when finished, with the corners folded as shown). Press them and hem them, then work a line of Stem Stitch immediately below them on all sides (except in the Cross Stitch areas). Finish the mat by pressing it on the wrong side into several layers of toweling, using a damp cloth.

DESIGNS FROM CHINA/Willow Pattern Pillow

Color, page 54.

MATERIALS NEEDED

Finished size, 16″ x 16″, design size 12½″ x 15″
#18 chenille needle
½ yd. blue cotton sailcloth or fine-linen fabric
Heavy twisted white cotton embroidery floss (use
    one whole strand) Persian wool in black, dark
    navy, marine blue, or medium blue (use one
    thread)

HOW TO GO ABOUT IT

Stretch the work into an embroidery hoop or canvas stretcher, 18″ x 18″. Enlarge the design photostatically or as on page 113 and trace it on the tracing paper with a fairly bold marker. Transfer the design by the method described below.

TRANSFERRING THE DESIGN BY BACK-LIGHTING

1. Stretch the fabric on a stretcher frame (see page 83).

2. With masking tape, hold your boldly traced design to the reverse side, close against the linen. Make sure the edges of the design run parallel with the lines you marked lightly with pencil on the linen to define its borders.

3. Arrange a goose-necked lamp or table lamp (the flexible kind are best) behind the stretcher frame, maneuvering the light in such a way that a clear silhouette of the design shines through the fabric.

4. Trace the pattern with a fine-tipped permanent marker, or India-ink pen. You will find that you frequently have to change the angle of the frame as you work so that the light silhouettes each area of design as you need it. Alternatively (though this is best for small designs), you could mount the fabric into a standing embroidery hoop and use the same method.

THE STITCHES TO USE

All tree trunks: Chain, Outlined Stem
Willow leaves: Open Fishbone
Tree: (left): Buttonhole
Trees (upper and lower right): French Knots outlined with Stem, Long and Short, Lazy Daisy
Pagoda: Squared filling, Slanting Satin, Back, Couching, Lazy Daisy, Padded Satin, Stem
Columns: Couching, Outlined Straight
Steps: Buttonhole, Split
Bridge and people: Chain, Satin
Ground: Buttonhole, French Knots, Satin, Padded Satin, Straight
Birds: Fishbone, Satin, Bullion Knots

Block the finished pillow face upward, following the instructions on page 186, and mount it with velvet backing and piping (or any other fabric you decide) according to the instructions on page 187.

ROUMANIAN STITCH/Spring Tapestry

Color, page 63.

MATERIALS NEEDED

½ yd. medium-weave natural linen (finished size, 15″ x 15″)

Persian wool in the following colors (use 3 threads):

1. Very pale green	9. Blue-gray
2. Light apple	10. Steel-gray
3. Medium apple	11. Pale silver-green
4. Bright apple	12. Medium blue-green
5. Light yellow	13. Dark blue-green
6. Bright yellow	14. Very dark blue-green
7. White	15. Dark kelly green
8. Violet gray	16. Light kelly green

HOW TO GO ABOUT IT

Enlarge the design and transfer it by using carbon (page 133) or back-lighting (page 143). Mount the fabric on stretcher-frame strips 18″ x 18″.

The design is worked almost entirely in Roumanian Stitch. Work the background vertically as shown below following the color-placement numbers marked on the design outline, and blending the color bands together by "splicing" the stitches as shown. For all the flowers and leaves, follow the direction lines shown on the diagram.

The colors are as follows: *snowdrops*, 7; *leaves*, 11 and 1; *aconites, lower flowers*, 6; *upper flowers*, 6 and 4; (Open Fishbone and Spiders' Webs); *leaves*, 3, 16, 15, 1, 2, and 5, *bog asphodel* (lower right), *flowers* 1, 8, and 9; (French Knots), *stems* 11; *leaves* 5, 11, 2, 3, 16, 8, 9; and 10.

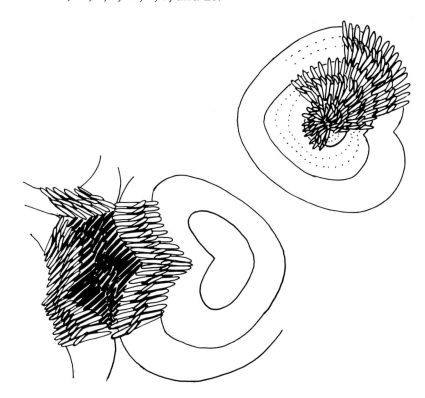

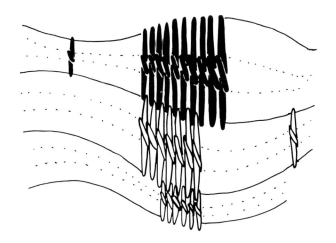

Top right: Roumanian stitch in a circle.
above: Two areas adjoining with small area of background between.
Left: Hills in background, with stitches dove-tailed in each row.

SPRING LAMBS

Color, page 63.

This design makes a pair with the Spring Tapestry and can be worked with the same materials and similar colors, except for the brilliant red strawberries.

The stitches are as follows:

Ground: Vertical Roumanian (as "Spring Tapestry")

Tree Trunks: Chain

Leaves (left to right): Buttonhole, Coral, Seeding, Chain, Stem, Fishbone, Padded Satin

Lambs: French Knots, Stem

Squirrel: Split, Stem, Coral

Flowers: Padded Satin, Stem

Strawberries: Squared filling, French Knots, Lazy Daisy

Both tapestries could be mounted as wall panels or used as pillows.

SATIN STITCH

Color, page 62.

MATERIALS NEEDED

¾ yd. heavy-weave linen, design size 16″ x 18″

Shag rug wool: light green, medium green, dark green, light blue, royal blue

Persian wool: aqua, medium aqua, peacock, light mauve, violet, purple, medium blue, pale blue, very pale blue

#18 chenille needle

HOW TO GO ABOUT IT

Transfer the design by carbon paper (page 133). Stretch the linen in a 36″ oval rug hoop or on a stretcher frame. Work "the sampler" entirely in Satin Stitch, following the direction lines indicated on the design opposite. The sampler includes:

Lower left leaf, butterfly: Block shading (bands of close Satin Stitch)

Left flower: Plain Satin (royal-blue shag rug wool)

Two flowers in aqua and violet: Satin Stitch with Split Stitch padding

Dragonfly wings: Satin Stitch with Stem Stitch outlines

Dragonfly body: Padded Satin Stitch

Stems: Stem Stitch and Open Fishbone

Flower centers: French and Bullion Knots

For precise colors, follow the color photo on page 62, or you may enjoy constructing your own color scheme.

CREWEL POINT TAPESTRIES

Color, pages 63, 65.

MATERIALS NEEDED

The two Garden of Eden pillows (pages 150 and 151) and the Morning Glory Trellis design opposite were all done on #12 canvas, using 3 threads of Persian wool and a #18 tapestry needle.

Finished size: 14″ x 14″

HOW TO GO ABOUT IT

The Morning Glory picture is shown in color in the center of page 63, and the Garden of Eden pillows are on page 64 (with a color closeup of a large panel of the same design on page 65). You can either follow the color schemes shown here or make up your own. The Garden of Eden pillows are particularly well suited to using your odd skeins of wool. Work them in rainbow shades of golds, oranges, reds, magentas, lilacs, and apple greens. The Morning Glories are all in blues, as you see, but they would be equally attractive in pinks and whites on the green leafy background.

All are examples of Satin Stitch on canvas, and all the stitches are worked either vertically or horizontally. Working in this way makes it easier to keep the edges smooth, so work diagonally only when it is absolutely essential, as for instance, around the butterflies' wings on page 150. The Straight Stitch described on page 110 is very effective when contrasted with an open canvas background. Alternatively, the background may be filled with Random Bargello (page 110), a long and short irregular stitch, which gives a good textured contrast with the smooth Satin Stitch.

The Morning Glories are all done in long and short Satin Stitches worked vertically on the canvas; the trellis is done in Satin Stitch worked *across* in the shortest angle; and the background is in Random Bargello, using various shadings of greens to give the effect of light and shade. The diagram makes it clear how the shadings are done and where the same colors repeat. You will find this kind of stitching satisfactorily quick and effective.

TURKEY WORK

MATERIALS NEEDED

Heavy, even-weave natural linen
Persian wool—black, gold, silver-gray, charcoal (use
  2 threads)
#18 chenille needle

HOW TO GO ABOUT IT

The bee is worked with bands of black and gold Turkey Work in his body—very raised, fluffy, and realistic.

Mount the design into an embroidery frame and first work the wings (pale silver-gray Split Stitch with darker outlines in Stem Stitch); head (black Satin Stitch), eye (padded Satin with white French Knots, and yellow Stem Stitch outline); and legs and antenna (black Back Stitch).

Then turn the body in the frame so that you can work long, horizontal lines of Turkey Work (see page 3). Start at the top and work parallel lines close together. Leave the loops about ¼″ long and pin them back if they get in your way as you work down, row by row.

Finally, trim the loops with scissors, shorter at the edges to round out the body. Fluff out the wool and trim to make the final result perfectly even. *Voilà*—your bee is ready to fly away!

SENTIMENTS IN STITCHES

MATERIALS NEEDED

Black felt-tipped marker
Tissue or tracing paper
Sewing cotton for basting
Wool or cotton floss for sewing the letters

HOW TO GO ABOUT IT

One of the best ways of getting letters on fabric, especially your signature, is to trace or write your name or message on tissue or tracing paper, using a felt-tipped marker. Mount the fabric in a frame and baste the tracing paper to it with long slanting stitches (as in the photo). Embroider the letters (Back Stitch seems ideal for a signature), working right through paper and fabric (second photo). Finally, tear the paper away—and as you see, a perfect signature! If you want to alter anything, all you have to do is unpick—there are no lines to make a mess of the background fabric.

WHEN ICICLES HANG BY THE WALL

AND DICK THE SHEPHERD BLOWS HIS NAIL

AND TOM BEARS LOGS INTO THE HALL

AND MILK COMES FROZEN HOME IN PAIL

SHAKESPEARE'S WINTER SONG

Color, page 68.

MATERIALS NEEDED

½ yd. fine-weave white linen
  Finished size, 14″ x 14″
Persian wool in the following colors (using one thread):

1. White	13. Dark apple-green
2. Black	14. Light gray
3. Red-orange	15. Medium gray
4. Orange	16. Dark gray
5. Medium rust	17. Flesh
6. Dark rust	18. Light yellow
7. Pale blue	19. Medium yellow
8. Medium blue	20. Deep yellow
9. Deep aqua	21. Light putty
10. Royal blue	22. Medium putty
11. Navy	23. Dark putty
12. Light apple-green	24. Light red-brown

#20 chenille or #4 crewel needles
Frame and stretcher strips, 18″ x 18″

HOW TO GO ABOUT IT

Assemble the stretcher strips, staple the design tightly, flat to the front. Enlarge the design and transfer it by back-lighting (page 143).

THE ORDER OF WORKING IS AS FOLLOWS:

All lettering: Back Stitch, 9
Sky: Laidwork, 7. Work across horizontally, wasting no thread on the reverse side. Where the lines are too long, break them by taking a Split Stitch. Cover the trees; they can be worked on top afterward.
Outline Hills: Back Stitch, 7; *fence,* 14
Trees: All trunks, Satin or Stem, 16; *branches,* Open Fishbone, 15
House (left): Laidwork, horizontally, 22; *outline roof,* Straight Stitch, 15 and 22; *top,* Back Stitch, 7; *windows,* Satin, 2; *horizontal band across house,* Satin, 21 and 23 alternating; *inn sign,* Satin, 5, Star, 4
Water barrel: Laidwork, 23, with Stem outlines, 16 (around barrel) and 23 and 1 (around top)
Pail: Laidwork, 14, top 14 and 1
Center houses: Laidwork 21; *windows,* Satin, 11; *outlines,* Straight, 15; *roof,* Laidwork and Back Stitch, 7
Center barns: Hay, Long and Short, 19, 21 and 20; *outlines,* Back Stitch, 22; *window at left,* Satin, 15
Figures: Woman: hat, Long and Short, 3, 5; *cape,* Split, 18 and 21, Outline, 15; *face,* Satin, 17; *skirt,* Chain, 10 and 9, Satin, 11, Chain, 8; *shoe,* Satin, 16. *Man: hat,* Satin, 13 and 12; *face,* Satin, 17; *arms,* Long and Short, 12 and 13; *jacket,* Satin, 4; *legs,* Satin, 10
Logs (on back and at feet): Satin, 24, *back* Stitch, 6
Rocks by Logs: Long and Short, 21, Satin, 24

When the picture is complete you can block it by dampening it right on the stretcher frame, mount it on a 14″ x 14″ stretcher, and frame it in any suitable frame.

AND LADY SMOCKS ALL SILVER WHITE

AND CUCKOO BUDS OF YELLOW HUE

DO PAINT THE MEADOWS WITH DELIGHT

WHEN DAISIES PIED AND VIOLETS BLUE

SHAKESPEARE'S SPRING SONG

Color, page 68.

MATERIALS NEEDED

½ yd. blue cotton sailcloth
    Finished size, 14″ x 14″
Persian wool in the following colors (use one strand:

1. White	11. Pale blue
2. Pale yellow	12. Blue-purple
3. Medium yellow	13. Light mint-green
4. Deep yellow	14. Grass green
5. Light orange	15. Light apple-green
6. Red	16. Medium apple-green
7. Brilliant pink	17. Light olive-green
8. Magenta	18. Medium olive-green
9. Lilac	19. Deep olive-green
10. Pale pink	20. Kelly green

#20 chenille or #14 crewel needle
Fanny or floor frame, or stretcher strips, 16″ x 18″

HOW TO GO ABOUT IT

Enlarge and transfer design, as on page 157.

ORDER OF WORKING

All lettering: Back Stitch, 3
Daffodil leaves: Slanting Satin, 13, 14, and 16
Daffodils: Petals, Long and Short, 4, 3, and 2; *centers,* Long and Short, 3, 4, and 5, Bullion Knots and French Knots, 2
Violet Leaves: Horizontal Laidwork, 20; *veins,* Split Stitch on top, 16; *stems,* Stem Stitch, 16
Violet flowers: Long and Short, 12, 9, and 8, Straight, 11
Daisy leaves: Long and Short, 3, 15, and 18
Daisies: Petals, Padded Satin, 6 and 1; *centers,* Padded Satin, 4
Buttercups: Padded Satin, 3 and 4; *centers,* French Knots, 15 and 16; *stalks,* Stem Stitch 16 and 15
Lady smocks (left): Padded Satin, 1, Bullion Knots, 14, French Knots, 7; *stems,* Stem Stitch, 20
Queen Anne's Lace (top): Star Stitch (radiate 6 straight Stitches from one central hole in 9 and 12; *stems,* Back Stitch 12
Two groups of right-hand flowers: French Knots (use two strands) 1, 15, and 2; *stems,* Stem Stitch, 16
Queen Anne's Lace (lower): Star Stitch, 15; *stems,* Back Stitch, 12
Lower leaves: Lazy Daisy with Stitch in the center, 16

Block and finish the picture as on page 157.

THINKING BIG

Color, page 69.

MATERIALS NEEDED

Linen twill, antique satin, upholstery satin, or other suitable hard-wearing fabric

English wools, Persian wools (use 1 or 2 threads)

#3 crewel needle, #18 chenille needle

HOW TO GO ABOUT IT

Enlarge and arrange the design on your chair, fitting it as shown on page 70. My design below exactly fits on top of the design opposite to form the chair *back* in the photo. Your chair *seat* design

could be adapted from repeats of the pattern on both pages. Once you have the pattern the correct size on tracing paper, transfer it according to the instructions on page 133 and 143, or if your fabric has a textured surface, the instructions on page 82.

Starting at the left, the flowers were worked in the following stitches:

1. Seeding, Stem Stitch, Chain, Satin, Fishbone
2. French Knots, Padded Satin, Whipped Spiders' Webs
3. Raised Stem, Outline Stem Stitch, French Knots, Bullions

4. Fishbone, French Knots
5. Close Herringbone, Padded Satin, Bullion Knots
6. Buttonhole (worked into a circle), Padded Satin, French Knots
7. Laidwork, Raised Stem, Fishbone, Padded Satin
8. Laidwork, tied with criss-cross lines, Padded Satin
9. Long and Short, French Knots, Satin

The leaves are worked in Chain, Satin, Buttonhole, Fishbone, and French Knots.

SENTIMENTS IN STITCHES/Animal New Baby Sampler

Color, page 77.

MATERIALS NEEDED

½ yd. fine white linen or cotton fabric
English crewel wool (use 1 and 2 threads)
#3 or #4 crewel needle

HOW TO GO ABOUT IT

The animals that are actual size on these pages may be traced and arranged around the message as shown in color on page 77. The order of working is best done as follows:

1. *Tendrils and stems*: Stem Stitch
2. *Faces of animals*: Work Long and Short, using three shades of brown and keeping all the stitches vertical, blending the colors.

3. *Features: Eyes and noses*, Satin Stitch; *whiskers*, Straight Stitches; *tails*, Knotted Pearl Stitches
4. *Bodies and clothes of animals*: Squared fillings with French Knots and Satin Stitch
5. *Baby's crib*: Work long horizontal stitches across the crib from one side to the other. Then work Raised Stem vertically on top.
6. *Bee and crib cover*: Turkey Work

Work the "message" in the center, transferring the traced arrangement, which you have worked out on graph paper, and following the instructions on page 155.

CREWEL POINT

Color, page 76.

MATERIALS NEEDED

#10 canvas (design size 12″ x 13″, finished size 15″
    x 16″)
Persian wool (use 3 threads)
#18 tapestry needle
Canvas stretchers, 18″ x 18″

HOW TO GO ABOUT IT

Enlarge the design on the opposite page, and trace it right through the canvas with a permanent marker (see page 49).

Follow the colors from page 76 and work all needlepoint stitches first (background, etc.), slightly overlapping the outlines of the areas to be worked in crewel. Then work most of the crewel stitches as if the canvas were fabric (not counting threads). Slightly superimpose crewel stitches over the backgrounds to cover the canvas and ensure a crisp outline. The stitches are as follows: on pages 110 to 112,

Background: Gros Point
Basket: Weaving (Couching around edges)
Pillow: Satin
Babies: Ears and faces, Buttonhole, with Long and Short
Coverlet: Turkey Work
Mother's dress: Scottish, Squared Filling
Apron: Brick
Baby's Dress: Chain (with *angora* wool!)
Mother's and baby's face: Long and Short
Ears: Baby's, Buttonhole; *Mother's*, Long and Short, Rope
Eyes: Satin and Seeding
Whiskers: Stem
Tails: Knotted Pearl

NOTE: Some of these stitches vary slightly from the color version. Use whichever you prefer.

THINKING BIGGER/Owl

Color, page 81.

MATERIALS NEEDED

½ yd. Brown Haitian cotton, design size 12″ x 14″

Rug wools in black, brown, white, antique gold, butter yellow, pale celadon green (use 1 thread)

Rug needle

Oval embroidery frame or 12″ floor frame

HOW TO GO ABOUT IT

Apply the design as described on page 82 (you can enlarge it first if you like—the drawing opposite is almost life size). Mount it in the embroidery frame and follow the order of working below:

Chest: Laidwork; vertical stitches in celadon with antique gold on either side, held flat with brown Open Fishbone worked on top afterward, as in the drawing

Wings: Laidwork vertical stitches in brown, held flat with Open Fishbone worked close together at wing tips, open toward shoulders (shown on right-hand wing)

Head: Long and Short, radiating around eyes, working from antique gold, to brown, to black. (Do not work black above eyes yet.)

Eyes: Vertical Satin Stitch, outlined first with yellow Stem Stitch then black Stem; white Seeding Stitch in center of each eye. Now work black stitches above each eye.

Top of head: Satin Stitch in celadon, starting with vertical stitches in the center, radiating them out above either ear as in the drawing

Beak: Work a single Satin Stitch in celadon outlined with black Straight stitches.

Upper chest: Work rows of white Stem Stitch, leaving each stitch loose to give a raised effect.

Feet: Bullion Knots in white

Tree: Stem Stitch outlines in brown

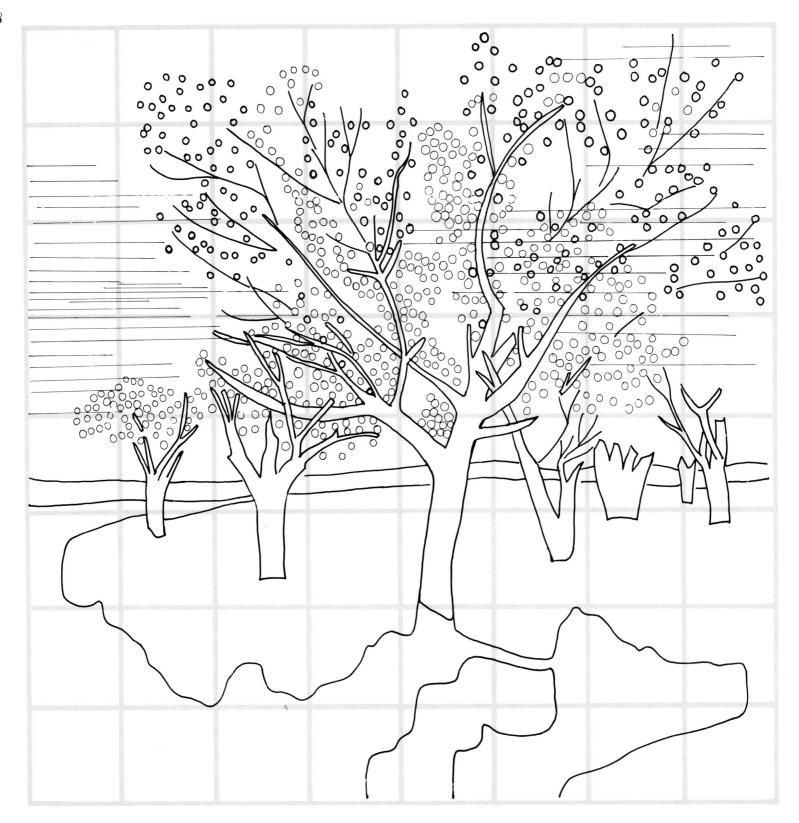

NEEDLEPAINTING

Color, page 84.

MATERIALS NEEDED

½ yd. blue sailcloth, denim or fine-weave linen
(design size 14″ x 14″)
Persian wools in the following colors:

Apple tree:	*Ground:*	*Sky:*
Pale blue	Dark green	White
Light-apple-green	Brilliant apple	
Medium apple-green	Light yellow-green	
Pale pink	Peach	
Brilliant red	Apricot	
Lavender	Yellow	
Royal blue	Light orange	
Charcoal	Medium orange	
	Orange-red	

#18 chenille needle
Stretcher strips, 16″ x 16″

HOW TO GO ABOUT IT

Mount the design on the stretcher strips, trace it from the drawing opposite, and transfer it, using the method on page 143 and following the instructions on page 84. "Paint" your picture with the colors listed above, threading several stitches with the different colors (as you see in the photo on page 83) so that you can use them as you go along.

The order of working is as follows:

Sky: Straight stitches, with Split stitches where lines are too long

Distant trees: Open Fishbone. Work them in royal blues, paler blues, and lavender.

Green hill (far away): Slanting Satin Stitch

Ground: Vertical Long and Short and Straight stitches. Under the green hill, upper left, work apricot Satin Stitch. Next, work basic ground in brilliant apple-green. In the foreground work apricot, peach, and orange. Superimpose Straight stitches, as in the colored photo on page 84, in lavender, yellow, red, and bright orange. Work fallen blossoms in white Raised Seeding.

Tree: Split stitches in red, gray, lavender for trunk, with red and blue branches in Straight Stitch.

Blossoms: Superimpose Raised Seeding stitches, leaving each stitch loose to form a raised "bump" on the fabric.

Block and frame the picture as described on page 188.

CROSS STITCH

Color, page 85.

Work on even-weave or patterned fabric, so that you can count out the design below (shown on page 85) and the alphabet opposite. Follow the instructions for Cross Stitch on page 20, always using a blunt needle to avoid splitting the threads, and to make a clear stitch.

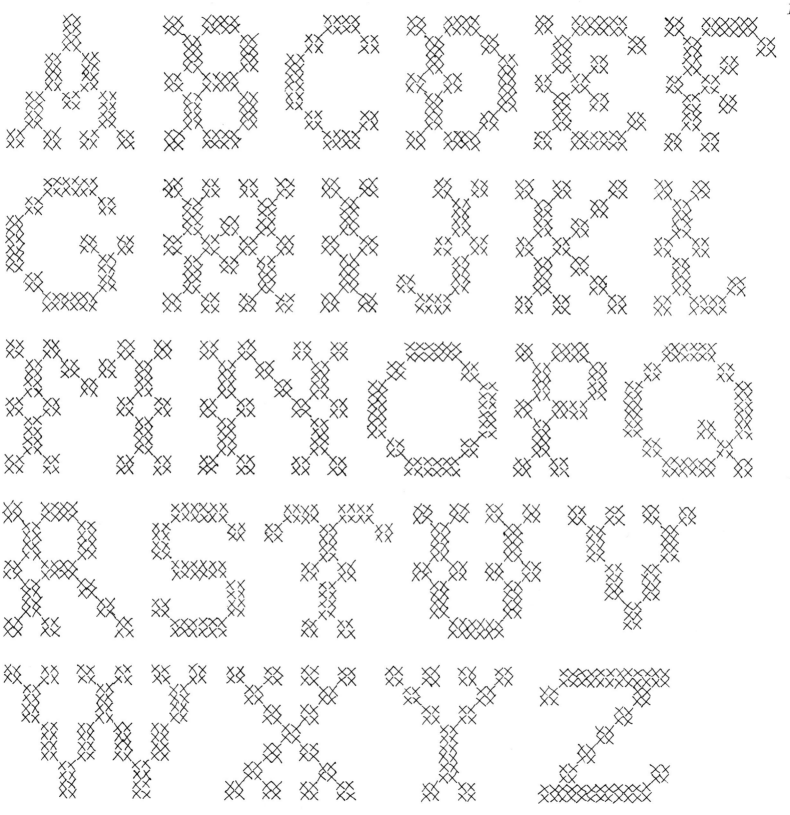

RIBBON PILLOW

Color, page 88.

MATERIALS NEEDED

1½ yd. length ribbons of varying widths
Eyelet ruffling for edging
Matching sewing thread
Tailor's chalk

HOW TO GO ABOUT IT

Machine- or hand-stitch the ribbons together, seaming each on the wrong side with right sides facing. Stitch together enough ribbons to give you a 10″ wide strip, 1½ yds. long. Cut a paper pattern 6½″ square, turn it, and pin it in the position on stitched ribbons shown by the black outlines on the drawing. Lay a ruler alongside the paper pattern and mark the lines with tailor's chalk. Mark 4 of these diamond shapes side by side, and cut along the lines you have marked, as in the drawing. Join the 4 squares as shown in the smaller drawing, seaming them right sides together with ½″ turnbacks, to make the first pillow. You can make a second pillow by joining the triangles left on either side, to form 4 squares, then join these squares as you did for the first pillow. Make them up with eyelet edging and velvet backs according to the instructions on page 186.

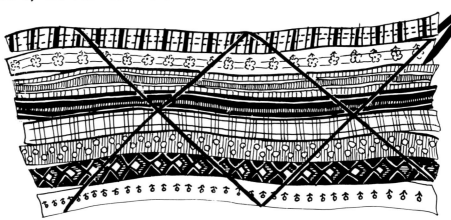

APPLIQUE OVEN MITT

MATERIALS NEEDED

Asbestos oven mitt
Felt
Matching or darker shades of Persian wool
Cotton embroidery floss

HOW TO GO ABOUT IT

Trace around the oven mitt, and cut it out in felt, half an inch larger all around. Make tracing paper patterns of the shapes opposite and cut them out in felt that coordinates or contrasts with the felt glove shape. (The center of the flower is made of circles of decreasing size, each one laid on top of the other.)

Using cotton, first hem the flower shape down, then each circle, then the stems, leaves, and other flowers. Work a French Knot in the center, outline the flower and leaf with Chain Stitch, and the buds with Buttonhole in wool. With right sides facing, sew the back and front of the mitt together, leaving it large enough so that when it is turned right side out, it will form a sleeve that will slip easily over the asbestos glove. Outline the seam with a line of Chain Stitch all around.

LITTLE YELLOW BASKETS

Color, page 92.

These marvelous little baskets can be used in December on your Christmas tree, in the Spring for your Easter decorations or year-round on your dining table for after-dinner mints.

MATERIALS NEEDED

1 Sheet of plastic canvas
1 Square of yellow felt
Orange and bright yellow acrylic yarn
#18 tapestry needle
½ yd. yellow gingham eyelet edging (optional)

HOW TO GO ABOUT IT

1. Cut the plastic in the following sizes, depending on which basket you want to make:
   a. Plain basket; 4 sides 2¼" x 1½", base 2¼", handle 4¾" x ½".
   b. Pincushion basket; 2 sides 1¼" x 2½", 2 sides 1½" x 1¼", base 2½" x 1½", handle ½" x 5".

   c. Strawberry workbox basket: 2 sides 2¼" x 4¾", 2 sides 2¼" x 3", base 3" x 4¾", handle ¾" x 8".

2. Using 2 threads in the needle, cover each piece with the weaving stitch following the diagrams. Work vertical stitches into each mesh with light yellow, then weave horizontally on every other mesh with dark yellow as in the diagram.

3. When you have completed all six pieces line them by lightly hemming a piece of felt to the back of each.

4. Join them together with one thread of yarn in the needle with the joining and binding stitch shown in the diagram.

5. Finish the raw edges of the handle again using the binding stitch. With one strand of wool use a running stitch to attach it to opposite sides of your basket.

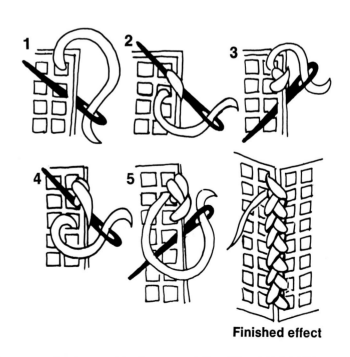

Finished effect

YELLOW BASKET PINCUSHION LID

To make the lid of the basket, trace the pattern shown here with ball point or pencil onto yellow gingham, leaving ½″ turnbacks all around. Work the strawberries (straight across from tip to leaves) in Long and Short stitch, shading from orange to magenta, or orange to pink or red. Highlight each one with a few white stitches in the center. Finally work 3 or 4 small black stitches, on top (as shown). Next work green Lazy Daisy stitches in all the small leaves, white Satin stitch in the flowers, and pale yellow French knots in each center. Use eyelet edging, or make a gingham ruffle by cutting a strip 1½″ x 24″, and folding it in half lengthwise. Gather the ruffle and baste it around the pillow on the right side, with the finished edge facing towards the center (as shown below). Stitch the back of the pillow on top, following the same basting lines, leaving one edge open for stuffing. Turn the pillow right side out, stuff firmly using shredded nylons, foam rubber or cotton batting, and sew the opening together with small invisible stitches.

Ruffle basted in position,
raw edges towards the outside.

To make the tiny pincushion basket, work on any green cotton or linen fabric; the leaves in Close Herringbone, the inner circle of the flowers in Rope Stitch, the dotted line around each in Stem Stitch in loose loops, and the dots in French Knots. Make a small, loose cushion with the finished embroidery, stuff it firmly, and ease it into the basket.

SMALL HOUSES

Color, page 92.

These little houses make ideal Christmas-tree decorations, could form a center piece for a table, or make a child's mobile.

MATERIALS NEEDED

1 sheet of plastic canvas (makes 3 houses)
9 colors of acrylic yarn
#18 tapestry needle

HOW TO GO ABOUT IT

Cut the plastic canvas according to the patterns below, carefully cutting out the mesh in the windows, leaving one bar crossing vertically and horizontally in the center of each. Outline the windows with white Tent Stitch (page 98), and cover the plastic bars with white acrylic, wrapping each closely. Work the 4 sides of the house in one brilliant acrylic color, the roof in the same stitch in another color. Join each piece together with the joining stitch shown on the preceding page. To ensure a square edge, hold both pieces of plastic to be joined back to back like a sandwich and sew through the two layers. Do not hold the pieces flat side by side to join them, or a rounded edge instead of a sharp one will be formed. Join the roof down the center, and stitch it invisibly to the rest of the house, giving the roof the proper overhang.

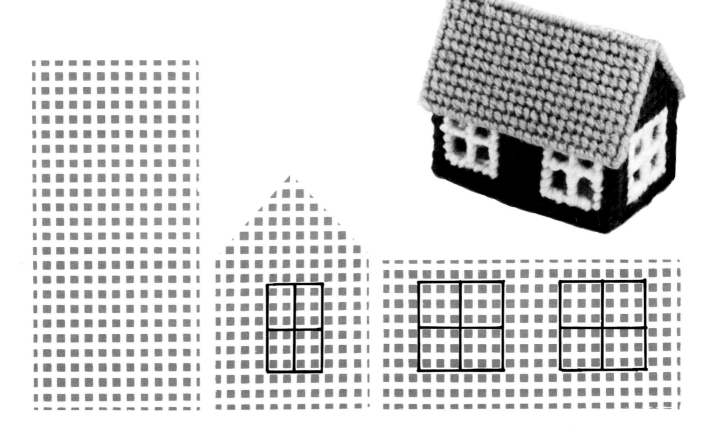

LARGE HOUSE

Color, page 92.

The large house can make an unusual handbag, or with a brick or weight inside it, can be used as a bookend or door stop.

MATERIALS NEEDED

2½ sheets of plastic canvas
Black felt
Persian or acrylic yarn in the following colors:

White	Sand	Apple-green
Light blue	Hot pink	Chartreuse
Dark blue	Red	Bottle-green
Black	Purple	Dark dull green
Yellow	Dark brown	Very dark green

#18 tapestry needle

HOW TO GO ABOUT IT

Cut the plastic according to the charts on the following pages (cut to size—no turnbacks). You can mark the position of the windows with a permanent marker, or count them out as you work, following the pattern.

Begin the thread with a knot on the reverse side. End off by running the thread through the stitching on the reverse.

ORDER OF WORKING

1. *Windows*: Work six black Cross Stitches in each, outline all around with white Tent Stitch.

2. *Shutters*: Work 10 horizontal Straight stitches in apple-green on either side of each window. Work a dark brown Straight Stitch on right of each shutter and top and base of window.

3. *Door*: Work like windows, in white Tent Stitch, with black Cross stitches on either side, dark brown Straight stitches.

4. Fill all *background* with horizontal Brick Stitch (page 106) in sand.

5. Work "flower garden" in crewel stitches on top—climbing roses, border flowers at base, and pine tree at right in Lazy Daisy stitches for the leaves, French Knots for flowers, using the brilliant colors.

6. Work all 3 other sides in the same way.

7. *Roof*: Work horizontal rows of Buttonhole Stitch (page 112), using dark dull green and dark brown alternately.

8. *Chimneys*: Work in vertical Brick Stitch, with shadows on roof in the same Buttonhole in dark blue.

Work a strip 58 holes x 7 holes in brown Tent Stitch to run across the top of the house. Repeat for the handle, 45 holes x 6 holes. Repeat for the clasp, 25 holes x 6 holes. Work this, then roll it up and stitch it to form a cylinder (stitch it firmly). Line with felt and join all pieces, leave upper-front section of roof open to form the opening for the bag. Stitch the handle and cylinder in place. Across from the cylinder, stitch a braid to the top of the roof. When this is looped around the cylinder it will keep the bag closed.

See pages 178-179 for diagrams.

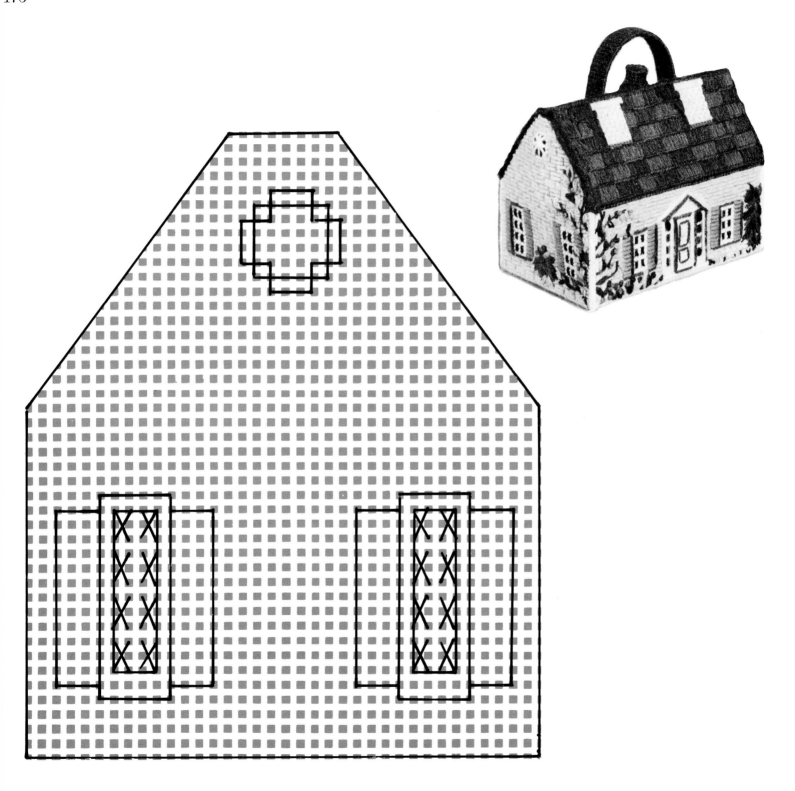

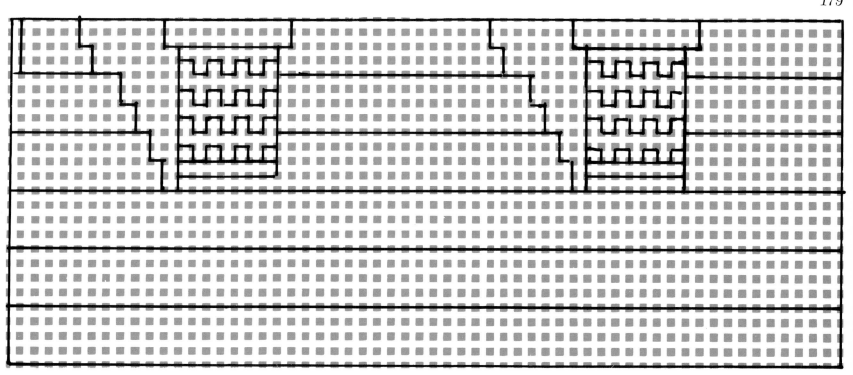

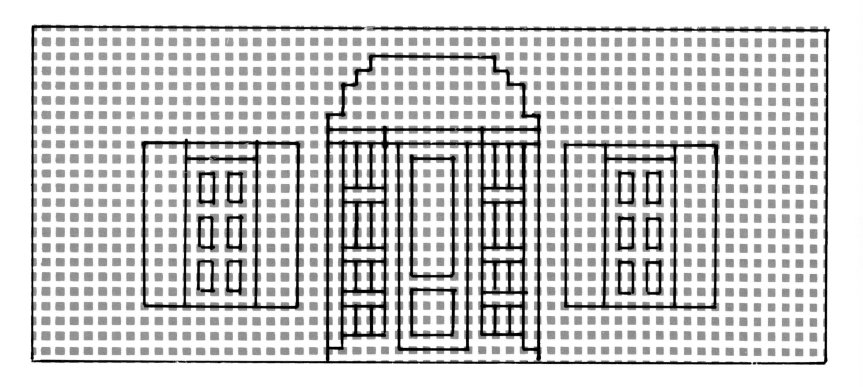

SHISHA

Color, page 93.

MATERIALS NEEDED

Indian mica or mirrors, "glitters," or
Mylar, or
Aluminum foil (heavy-duty) and cardboard disks
Persian wool in brilliant colors or cotton
    embroidery floss
#4 crewel needle
Bluejeans

HOW TO GO ABOUT IT

Launder the bluejeans to soften them, open up the side seams for ease of working, and enlarge and transfer the design, according to the method on page 82 or page 143.

Put the jeans into an embroidery frame and begin by working in all the mirrors, following the instructions on page 33. Work the same Shisha Stitch to fill the leaf or bird shapes *behind* the mirrors, then work all outlines and stems with Chain Stitch. The embroidery may be done in cotton floss or wool, in brilliant or in muted colors, according to your fancy! The work shirt on page 182 was done in the same way.

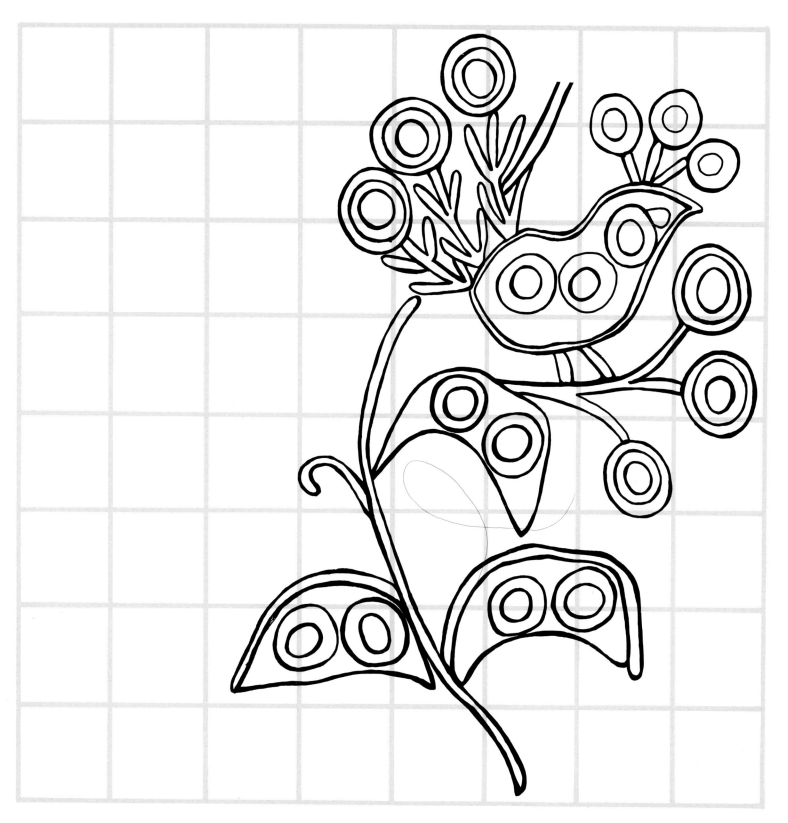

REVERSE APPLIQUE TABLE MAT

MATERIALS NEEDED

Felt in various colors
Matching cotton thread
#4 crewel needle

HOW TO GO ABOUT IT

Cut a rectangle of felt the color you want the top of your table mat to be.

Fold it in half, in half again, and in half one more time. Then cut circles and triangles out of the folded felt as in the diagram. (If you wish, practice with paper first.)

Open up your cut felt and lay it on another color. Pin it down as in the drawing, and cut away your next layer, inside the shapes, leaving a border of the new color exposed all around. Continue, layer by layer, until the final color makes the base. Hem each one down to the next, and edge the mat with a binding of one of the predominant colors.

ORIENTAL GOLD

Color, page 96.

MATERIALS NEEDED

Wooden hinged jewel box
Red suede-cloth fabric

Japanese gold thread
Sequins
Maltese sewing silk
Beeswax
Sobo glue
#4 crewel needle

HOW TO GO ABOUT IT

Enlarge and trace the pattern to fit your box. Mount it on stretcher frames or into a hoop large enough not to mark the fabric and transfer it by the methods on page 82 or page 143.

Thread the needle with Maltese silk, wax it by pulling it two or three times through the beeswax, and use it to couch down a double row of gold thread following the instructions on page 33. With practice, your couching will become very smooth. Pay particular attention to turning corners and joining in another line. Sew down the sequins wherever the design indicates with 2 or 3 stitches going down into the center. Mount the box by first padding the top slightly, then gluing the embroidery in place, starting with the lid. Cut off excess with a razor blade *after* all sides have been glued in place. Although the suede cloth will not fray, the raw edges should be taken to the inside of the box for a professional finish.

BLOCKING

Before blocking any article, test a corner of the work to make sure that both wool and background fabric are fast color.

Crewel and crewel point should be blocked face upward to allow the raised stitches to stand out. Needlepoint should always be placed face downward for a smooth effect.

Needlepoint needs special attention in blocking because sometimes the stitches are apt to pull the design very much out of shape. If your work does not need cleaning, block it before you wet it—it will be easier to handle. Lay it out, right side up on a board or an old table, which has first been covered with a sheet. Use a chip or particle board, not plywood, otherwise the tacks will be hard to hammer in. Then with carpet tacks (not thumbtacks, which are not strong enough), nail down the four corners first, measuring the opposite sides to see that they are even and making sure the corners are true right angles. You can use the two sides of the board or table to guide you by placing the

first two sides of the design close to them to begin with, and you will find it best to pull the design out firmly with pliers to make sure it is really taut.

Don't worry if the tacks stain the canvas with rust marks—this will be cut away with the "turning" (the extra canvas that disappears in the seams). Then nail down four more tacks, one in the center of each side, and then eight more in the spaces between. Continue round and round, adding in this way more tacks until they are about $\frac{1}{4}''$ apart. Take a cloth and a bowl of water and thoroughly soak the needlework, then allow it to dry in its own time. When it is thoroughly dry, take it up, and if it is not being mounted immediately, roll it round a cardboard tube with the right side of embroidery outward so that the stitches are not crushed against one another.

If your needlework needs cleaning, soak it in cold water in the bathtub before blocking and wash gently with a cake of Ivory soap (having first tested with soap to make sure it will not run).

ASSEMBLING PILLOWS

Pillows may be made up with lace or eyelet embroidery edgings, with pipings or with boxings (a narrow band of fabric stitched between back and front to give the pillow a "box" effect). When pillows are made up without a boxing they are generally referred to as "knife-edge."

In the instructions below, simply substitute boxing or whatever kind of edging you are using for the lace; the directions will be the same:

1. Make a pattern for your pillow, adding ½″ seam allowance beyond your finished size.

2. To make a pillow "form" (inner pillow), following your pattern, cut out two shapes in muslin for back and front.

3. Stitch all around, leaving a 4″ opening. Turn right side out and fill with stuffing. Hand-stitch opening closed.

4. Gather lace, or make piping (covering cord with strip of bias-cut fabric and stitching close below cord).

5. Following your pattern, cut out yarn-embroidered front and the back of your pillow.

6. Place the gathered lace in position around the border of embroidery, lining up the edges with ruffle toward the center so that there will be ¼″ of lace in the seam. Sew it in position, holding the ruffle toward the inside right sides facing (see diagram on page 175).

7. With right sides facing, pin pillow back to front and ruffle.

8. Now, stitch together (front, back and ruffle), allowing ½″ in seam and leaving a 4″ opening.

9. Turn right side out and insert pillow form. Hand-stitch opening closed.

TO MOUNT THE BOLSTER

Block the needlepoint (page 186) and seam it, right sides facing, to form a tube.

Gather 2 rectangles of velvet, 3″ x 14″, at the top and bottom of the longest edge. Seam the two ungathered edges together. Now draw up one edge very tightly, the other one less, to form a flat circle. Make the velvet pipings 14″ long, by covering the cord with a narrow strip of cross-cut velvet and stitching it closely below the cord. Join each carefully to form a 14″ circle. Sew each

around the right side of the gathered circles, (raw edges toward the outside circumference). Attach each to either end of the bolster, right sides facing. Leave one end sufficiently open to enable you to turn it right side out.

Before stuffing, attach a long piece of strong linen or nylon thread to one of the covered buttons, and thread it through from the center of one gathered end, through the bolster to the other gathered end. Leave the thread hanging there until the bolster is tightly stuffed, sew the opening for the stuffing together, draw up the nylon thread very tightly and firmly attach it to the second button.

NOTE: If you feel your nimble fingers are best suited to the needlepoint only, give it out to a professional upholsterer!

TO MOUNT THE MIRROR FRAME

MATERIALS NEEDED

Foam core board
Masking tape
Rubber cement
Mirror, 10″ x 12″
"Silver Strips" frame, 1 pair 18″, 1 pair 20″

HOW TO GO ABOUT IT

1. Block your mirror frame embroidery according to the instructions on page 186.

2. With a knife or heavy scissors cut one piece of foam board 18½″ x 20½″. Cut a second piece the same size with 9½″ x 11½″ opening for the mirror, using your graph paper template. Cut around the needlework, leaving 1½″ turnbacks all around the outer edge and mount it on the foam core board turning back the outer edges and holding them flat with masking tape. Now cut 4 diagonal slits from the center to the 4 corners of the mirror opening, cutting ½″ short of each corner to prevent fraying. Now fold the four flaps to the back of the board, trim them, leaving 1½″ turnbacks, and hold them firmly in place with masking tape. The embroidery should be stretched firmly to the board—no wrinkles!

3. Lay your mounted embroidery on top of the other piece of foam core board, and making sure the two are aligned at the outer edges, run a pencil around the opening for the mirror, which is framed by your embroidery. Lift off the embroidery and glue the mirror into the correct position you have just marked on the board, using Duco cement.

4. With masking tape, hold the 2 pieces firmly together at the edges, and frame them in the silver strip frame, as shown in the photograph on page 35.

For information on any of the hard-to-find articles in this book, such as gold thread, French or English wool, pre-mounted handbags, tennis-racquet covers for needlepoint, etc., please write to Erica Wilson Needleworks, 717 Madison Avenue, New York, New York 10021.

INDEX OF STITCHES